Medieval Churches
of
West Yorkshire

Peter Ryder

photographs by Paul Gwilliam

ISBN 1 870453 17 4

British Library Cataloguing-in-Publication Data.
A catalogue record for this book is available from the British Library.

Published by: West Yorkshire Archaeology Service on behalf of the Archives, Archaeology and Trading Standards Sub-Committee of the West Yorkshire Joint Services Committee

Printed by: Witley Press, Hunstanton, Norfolk

Editor: Stuart Wrathmell, assisted by Chris Philo
Sub-editor and DTP: Lyn Turner

Photography: Paul Gwilliam, with additional photographs by Bob Yarwood (**11, 13, 23, 29**), Tony Wilmott (**30**) and Steve Wager (**173**), and from the organisations cited above in the statement of copyright.

Line drawings: Chris Philo, with additional drawings by Jon Prudhoe (**12** and glossary illustrations), Peter Brears (**16**), Andrew Swann (**169-71, 174-75**), Sue Nelson (**178**, no. 6) and Paula White (glossary plan).

Contents

List of Illustrations

Numbers which appear in bold in the text refer to the illustrations

Preface

In 1987 the West Yorkshire Archaeology Service began a major field survey of medieval churches in the county. The investigation, carried out by Peter Ryder, was intended to provide an archaeological perspective on buildings which had, by and large, escaped detailed study. It aimed to establish a 'fabric history' for structures whose dating had previously depended upon the form and style of architectural features, mainly doorways and windows. The survey also had two other objectives: first to enable better informed decisions to be made on future proposals for church reordering, refurbishment and restoration; and secondly, to encourage the proper provision for archaeological recording and building preservation. The work was carried out over a period of two years, and involved an assessment of fixtures, fittings and churchyard monuments, as well as the buildings themselves. It entailed a limited amount of documentary research, focusing upon antiquarian descriptions of buildings since demolished or radically altered; it also included an assessment of the archaeological potential of each church site.

The survey was the outcome of discussions with Richard Morris of the Council for British Archaeology (CBA). A much more elaborate project on the same theme had been mooted some ten years earlier, encompassing not only measured surveys of buildings, but also extensive documentary research to locate churches and church sites within their medieval communities and in the landscape. Although some progress had been made by CBA researchers using modest funding from the former Metropolitan County Council, it was agreed that a less ambitious survey – but one making more effective use of available expertise – was required. This was the genesis of Peter Ryder's survey and Paul Gwilliam's subsequent photographic survey, which were both funded entirely by the West Yorkshire Archives and Archaeology Joint Committee on behalf of the district councils.

This volume, which draws its detailed information from the survey, is based primarily upon the churches now within West Yorkshire which were centres of 'ancient parishes' (see illustration 1).[1] These are described and discussed irrespective of the extent of post-medieval demolition and rebuilding. In addition, a number of subordinate chapels are included. Some, such as Woolley, later became parish churches themselves; others, like the one at Lotherton Hall, remain dependent chapels. This publication concerns itself with such buildings where a substantial amount of the medieval fabric survives (as at Heptonstall), or where (as at Beeston) the medieval chapel was recorded in some detail before being demolished and replaced.

There were, however, many other medieval chapels in the county of which nothing is presently known other than an occasional documentary reference: Ripponden chapel, for example, which was built in the 1460s; or a chapel of ease in Bradford which stood beside Bradford Beck in the mid-15th century; or Baildon, where a chapel is documented before the year 1200. Also omitted are the many

---

1   As defined in the county survey: M. Faull and S.A. Moorhouse, *West Yorkshire: An Archaeological Survey to AD 1500* (1981)

domestic chapels, whether or not they are marked by surviving structural remains. Pontefract Priory was granted a chapel in their manor of Whitwood (Featherstone parish) in the late 12th century, on condition that they did not allow parishioners access to it. Nothing is known of the structure of that particular building, but the remains of what is traditionally identified as the chapel of Rothwell Manor can still be seen. So, too, can the 15th-century chapel built within Calverley Hall.[2]

The Archaeology Service owes particular thanks to Richard Morris for his help and encouragement in the planning and implementation of the survey, and to Warwick Rodwell for reading and commenting upon this volume. Peter Ryder thanks Kate Mason, David Parsons and Roberta Gilchrist for their help in the investigation of particular churches; as well as Robin and Cathy Sermon and Jonathan and Heather Foote for their hospitality during his fieldwork. Additional information and advice was provided by Ian Roberts, Andrew Swann, Peter Thornborrow, Robin Turner, Bob Yarwood and Stuart Wrathmell of the Archaeology Service, and by Lawrence Butler and John Hunter. Paul Gwilliam was assisted in the photographic survey by Michael Fossick. The many old illustrations – engravings, drawings, watercolours and early photographs – which were photographed or redrawn for use in this volume, appear by courtesy of numerous organisations and individuals, including: City of Wakefield Metropolitan District Council (Wakefield Museums, Galleries and Castles), Kirklees Metropolitan Council (Cultural Services), Leeds Leisure Services department of Leeds City Council (Leeds City Museums and Leeds City Libraries), University of Leeds (Brotherton Library, Special Collections), West Yorkshire Archive Service and Peter Thornborrow. Above all, however, the Archaeology Service gratefully acknowledges the help of the incumbents and wardens of all the churches featured in this volume, not only through the provision of early illustrations in their care, but also for their unfailing assistance during the investigation and recording of West Yorkshire's medieval churches.

John D. Hedges
County Archaeologist

St Mary's Luddenden: an old engraving depicting one of several chapels founded in the extensive parish of Halifax towards the end of the Middle Ages. The present church building is no earlier than the 19th century.

2   RCHM(E), *Rural Houses of West Yorkshire, 1400-1830*, Supplementary Series 8 (1986, Royal Commission on the Historical Monuments of England, West Yorkshire Metropolitan County Council), 193-94

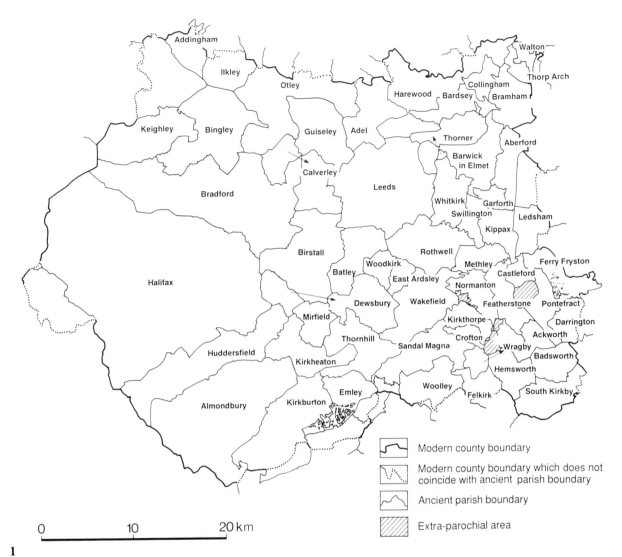

1

The medieval parishes of West Yorkshire.

Legend:

- Modern county boundary
- Modern county boundary which does not coincide with ancient parish boundary
- Ancient parish boundary
- Extra-parochial area

The brief gazetteer entries which appear in this volume are summaries of the full survey descriptions and interpretations; these, along with ancillary documentation and full source references, are available for public consultation in the West Yorkshire Sites and Monuments Record, housed at 14 St John's North, Wakefield WF1 3QA.

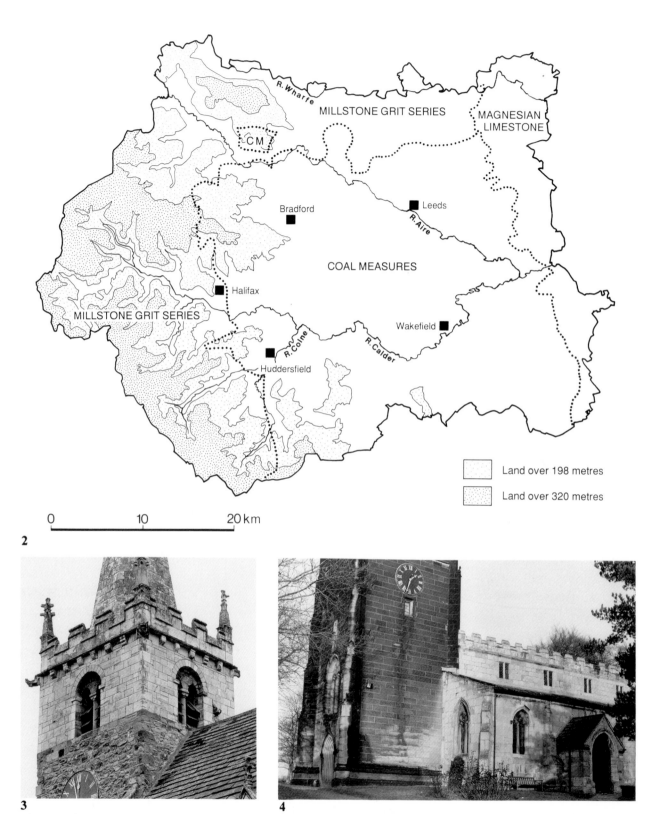

2

3

4

The varied geology of West Yorkshire (2) is illustrated by the diversity of stone types in its medieval churches. Ledsham (3) has a sandstone Anglo-Saxon porch overbuilt by a limestone Norman belfry. Swillington (4) has a tower with Victorian gritstone facings attached to the medieval limestone church.

CHAPTER ONE

The Medieval Parish Churches of West Yorkshire

Introduction

The modern county of West Yorkshire, carved out of the old West Riding in 1974, is not renowned for its ancient parish churches. Its medieval churches did not attract a great deal of attention from the antiquaries of the 19th century; as a group they were spoken of disparagingly as being almost all in one style, the 'Perpendicular' of the 15th and early 16th centuries, and being mostly built from the coarse Pennine gritstones which did not permit the sculptor much scope for the carving of elaborate detail (**2, 3, 4**).

These criticisms are partly true. The late medieval prosperity of the area – resulting from, amongst other factors, the growth of the textile industry – did see many churches being rebuilt or, more frequently, remodelled around an older core. West Yorkshire churches, at least those in the west of the county, are generally lacking in high-quality carving. However, the recent survey by the Archaeology Service has shown that the survival rate of medieval fabric in the county's churches is remarkably high, especially for an area marked by industrial and urban expansion in the 18th and 19th centuries. Out of 55 medieval parish churches in what is now West Yorkshire, no less than 49 are represented by *in situ* medieval structural remains; one can compare this with a similar number of parishes in rural south-east Wiltshire,[1] where over a quarter of the medieval churches were completely rebuilt in the mid-19th century alone.

The recent survey has demonstrated how little has actually been known about the older church buildings in the area. Many can now be shown to have far more varied and complex structural histories than their external appearances at first suggest; remains of Anglo-Saxon fabric, previously recognised in only three churches in the county, may in fact survive in over a dozen. We now know that the late medieval remodellings, which many of the churches underwent, took place phase by phase as earlier parts of the building were replaced. At this period the hands of individual designers can perhaps be traced in the distinctive west towers, and in details of arcades and parapets.

The survey begins with a discussion of the ways in which one can assess and interpret an old church. This is followed by a series of chapters which attempt to draw out some of the principal themes of church building development, dealt with period by period. The case studies of Featherstone and Tong churches are followed by a gazetteer of all 69 churches and chapels examined. In addition to the structures themselves, church monuments, fittings and furnishings,

---

1 RCHME, *Churches of South-East Wiltshire* (1987, Royal Commission on the Historical Monuments of England)

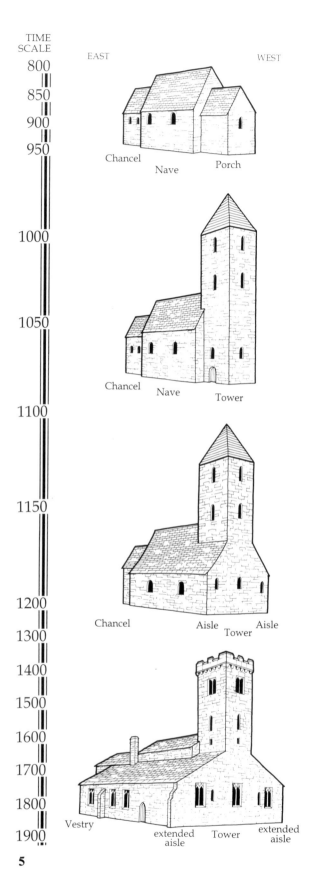

TIME
SCALE

800
850
900
950

1000

1050

1100

1150

1200
1300
1400
1500
1600
1700
1800
1900

EAST   WEST

Chancel   Nave   Porch

Chancel   Nave   Tower

Chancel   Aisle   Aisle
                    Tower

Vestry   extended   Tower   extended
                    aisle   aisle

5

The development of Bardsey church over a thousand years is shown on the left (**5**): the building has been successively heightened, with the construction of a tower, widened (in two stages) by the addition of aisles, and lengthened at the east end. Much of the structural development can be seen in the west wall (**6**) which contains the evidence for the Anglo-Saxon porch, the Late Saxon tower, the Norman aisles and the late medieval enlargement of those aisles. The upper part of the tower was remodelled in the later Middle Ages.

6

stained glass, fonts and bells are all the subject of brief accounts, sufficient to demonstrate the wealth of the region, and the number of fields in which research still needs to be carried out.

Studying an old church

It is a common fallacy that archaeologists are interested only in what lies below the ground surface. Any ancient feature or artefact, from a cathedral down to a scrap of pottery, is a document-without-words which can be read or interpreted to reveal information about the period and the people that produced it. The more complex the feature or artefact, the more complex the ways in which the archaeologist needs to look at it in order to gain from it the maximum amount of information.

In this way a medieval parish church, which is very often the oldest building to survive within a village or town, can be viewed as a document to be read. Since the 19th century, the study of such buildings has been very much the preserve of the architectural historian rather than the archaeologist; often the only published accounts of churches are in the pages of architectural studies such as Sir Nikolaus Pevsner's famous *Buildings of England* series. What is now the traditional means of examining a church in terms of its architectural features can, however, result in a serious misreading of its history. This is perhaps best demonstrated by citing a theoretical example.

A church may be described in such terms as: 'aisled nave with Perp. arcades, chancel with E.E. lancet windows'. Interpreting the architectural shorthand, this would imply that the nave arcades (and perhaps both nave and aisles) were built in the Perpendicular style of the 15th or early 16th century, but that the chancel was presumably earlier in that it had Early English windows in the style popular through the first half of the 13th century. It is very common to find churches assessed in print in this manner; one might call this a 'Level 1' assessment, where architectural features are taken at their face value in that they are assumed both to be genuine (i.e. their style is a correct guide to their date), and to be of the same date as the part of the building in which they are found.

In practice, this Level 1 approach almost invariably leads to serious problems, and to many misinterpretations of old buildings (not just churches). Architectural features are in fact often inserted in older walls (**7, 8**): sometimes this is quite apparent from the way in which their dressed stonework relates to the coursing of the masonry of the wall, but sometimes it is difficult to tell. Looking at the masonry, or fabric, of the wall itself may help. Whilst the details of an architectural feature – the mouldings of an arch, or the Norman ornament round a doorway – may be quite distinctive, and recognisable to anyone familiar with basic architectural text books, fabric types vary from area to area, as well as from period to period. One needs to look not only at the type of stonework – rubble, ashlar, roughly squared stone – but at the way the corners of the building are treated: the type of angle quoin – the stone blocks used to make the corner – is often important; the thickness of the walls may also be very significant. The nave with its 'Perp. arcades' may have rubble walls 0.60m thick with massive well-squared angle quoins laid in what would be termed 'side-alternate' fashion. These features of the walling would, taken together, be good evidence that the wall itself was of Anglo-Saxon date, and at least four centuries older than the inserted arches.

Turning to the chancel of our theoretical church, with its 'E.E. lancet windows', a close inspection might show that the stone dressings surrounding the windows looked suspiciously well

7

8

A close look at the south wall of Ledsham nave (7) demonstrates the complexity of the archaeological information contained in the walls of some old churches. The explanatory drawing (8) shows the positions of two blocked windows which preceded the present 15th-century window.

squared, as if machine-cut, although the stone might be quite weathered. Are they medieval or Victorian? In some areas, especially industrial ones, softer stones can weather to a very 'ancient' appearance within a century. In 1847-48 Sir George Gilbert Scott replaced the old facade of the Wakefield Bridge Chantry with a replica carved in Caen stone; by 1939, when it had to be renewed again, the facade was in a far worse state of decay than the original had ever been. So are we looking at a 13th-century lancet window in which the dressings have been recut during a 19th-century restoration, one in which the medieval stonework has simply been replaced, or a 19th-century window imitating a 13th-century style? This is when a visit to the Diocesan or County Record Office becomes necessary, to trace old descriptions, and, even better, any illustrations of the church before the Victorians 'restored' it. If we are lucky we might find an old print, or a 'prior to proposed alterations' elevation drawing which shows that instead of lancet windows, the chancel used to have simple three-light windows in a style somewhere between Perpendicular and Tudor. In the mid-19th century, Early English Gothic was seen as the high-point of Christian architecture, and the most fitting style for a church; the three-light windows would have been adjudged 'debased' or 'of domestic character' and unfit for a place of worship. So what was the date of the original chancel prior to its restoration? The fabric here might be of large, well-squared gritstone blocks, with a coarse diagonal tooling; this and the wave-like moulding of the plinth at the foot of the wall (a 'minor' architectural feature often ignored by visitors) would confirm that the chancel had in fact been rebuilt sometime in the early 16th century. Further documentary research might show that in

4

the early 1700s a visiting antiquary recorded stained glass in the chancel containing coats of arms of local families in a combination which, historical records will show, would have been used only around 1520.

Thus a Level 1 approach will give some easy answers, although they may well be wrong ones! Turning to the opposite extreme, one could subject a church to a full archaeological examination (which we might term 'Level 3'), studying all parts of its fabric and features in detail. This is only really possible when the above-ground structure of a building is dismantled and its below-ground archaeology fully excavated. This of course rarely happens – an opportunity might arise when a church has to be reconstructed on a new site – and if it did would consume a great deal of time and effort. St Martin's church at Wharram Percy, North Yorkshire, is perhaps the most thoroughly examined medieval church in the north of England, having been excavated, in conjunction with the site of the medieval village which it once served, over a number of years. Its above-ground fabric has been closely inspected and recorded during consolidation,[2] although it has not actually been taken down. The result of all this is that twelve constructional phases have been recognised in the church, of which only four or five had been surmised previously. Yet a considerable number of major questions still remain unanswered: for example, in its early 12th-century form the church was obviously intended to have had a large west tower, but it still remains uncertain whether such a tower was actually built. Another problem which a more superficial study would not have uncovered was that quite a number of the architectural features of the church had been reused during later alterations and extensions; the windows in the side walls of the nave, for instance, came from the original aisles, being moved when these were demolished and the church was reduced in size.

In the course of the survey on which this book is based, a 'Level 2' examination of West Yorkshire churches was the aim, intermediate between a superficial assessment based on architectural style and a full archaeological examination. Features such as fabric type, joints between different types of masonry, and changes in wall thickness were recorded, in addition to the form and position of the various architectural features. Few churches could be examined in as close detail as they deserved: internal wall faces are often either hidden by plaster, especially frustrating in the case of a church like Otley; or they are relatively inaccessible, such as the upper parts of the nave walls at Halifax, which really need scaffolding and proper lighting for a detailed inspection. However, the principle of looking at the whole building rather than just its architectural features paid dividends in many cases, most notably in the identification of probable pre-Conquest fabric in quite a number of churches; it also has the less helpful consequence of raising more questions than it provides answers for, and on more than one occasion provoked doubts as to the validity of a long-accepted interpretation of a particular church fabric.

The basic tool in a Level 2 study is simply a good visual inspection; one does not need to be an archaeologist to look at a building in this way. An accurate ground plan of a church, when available, is also a great help, as are elevation drawings. More sophisticated forms of investigation are being used today, such as types of photography which can detect remains of wall paintings beneath overlying plaster, dendrochronology by which timbers can be dated from their tree-ring patterns, and chemical analyses of mortars, or petrological analyses of stone types.

---

2   R.D. Bell, and M.W. Beresford, *Wharram. A Study of Settlement on the Yorkshire Wolds, III. Wharram Percy: the Church of St Martin* (1988, Society for Medieval Archaeology Monograph 11, London)

The end result of a detailed inspection of an old church is the reconstruction of its building history, knowing what changes took place and, roughly, when they happened (**5, 6**). The question that inevitably follows, and one that is often very hard to answer, is why the changes took place. Most churches, like old houses that remain inhabited, are 'living' buildings, still being used for their original purpose, and thus quite distinct from the usual archaeological site or artefact, the function of which has long since ceased. The purposes of the different parts of a house are relatively easy to reconstruct; people's physical needs are unchanging and their structural expression is usually readily recognisable. A kitchen is identified by its fireplace, the position of the high table in the hall by the remains of the decorated canopy above it, and the garderobe or latrine by its drain or pit.

Reconstructing the functions of various parts of a church is a different matter. Here the changing plan, features and furnishings all relate to forms of ceremony and liturgy which aimed to serve the spiritual needs of the parishioners. Such functions are far less readily tangible in terms of archaeological evidence than are the domestic arrangements of a dwelling house. The difference in plan between Anglo-Saxon churches, with their series of *porticus* or separate small chambers flanking the main body of the church, and Norman churches with full-length aisles, implies some change in how churches were used; although contemporary writings provide some valuable clues, we know relatively little about forms of service so long ago. More readily understandable is the obvious change between the plan of the medieval church with its long chancel, and the simple broad rectangle of the 18th-century 'preaching box' church. In the first the emphasis was upon the Sacrament, with the celebrant at the altar remote from the congregation in the nave; in the second it was upon the Word, with the pulpit the most prominent feature. All these changes are the product of a process which is still continuing; the return to ritual which accompanied the revival of medieval architectural forms in the Victorian period, and more recent liturgical reforms resulting in the reordering of many churches, with the altar being brought into the crossing or nave, are just further chapters of the same story. This publication concentrates on the medieval churches of West Yorkshire, and on the surviving monuments and furnishings of that period, but a church cannot really be understood apart from the people who built and used it; the visitor should bear in mind that the structural history of every church building is simply the visible expression of a worshipping community which has been in existence for, in most cases, more than 1000 years.

CHAPTER TWO

The First Eight Centuries

Within the last 20 or 30 years archaeological research has shed much new light on the early centuries of Christianity in Britain; long-established ideas and 'popular history', based on a scatter of documentary references, traditions and assumptions, are having to be revised.

Those who first brought the Christian faith to these islands are shadowy figures, and will probably always remain so. What is clear is that the new religion was well established, and being widely practised, in the Roman Britain of the 3rd century. Worship, and whatever ritual was in use at this time, seems to have taken place within private houses; the establishment of churches and chapels as distinct public buildings probably took place only after the end of the reign of the persecuting Emperor Diocletian (284-305). By the mid-4th century the country had been divided up into several dioceses, each with its own bishop. Excavations in the Roman cities of Canterbury, Colchester and Lincoln have recently revealed substantial buildings identified as churches. There is also growing evidence that many pagan temples were converted into churches at this time, as almost certainly took place at the London Temple of Mithras, and possibly also at the great temple beside the sacred spring and baths at Bath. In the romanised parts of Britain many of the present parish churches may well stand on the same sites as their 4th and 5th-century predecessors; the close association between parish churches and Roman villa sites (several hundred instances are known) can now be seen as evidence of the church having developed from a Christian chapel or christianised garden shrine which belonged to the villa, rather than being a later 'planting' beside a ruined villa which simply happened to provide a useful source of building material.

9

Roman stonework reused in Anglo-Saxon churches: part of a pagan altar at Ledsham (9), and one of two similar altars fashioned into window heads at Ilkley (10).

10

11

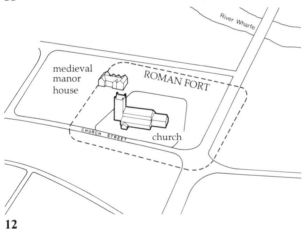

The medieval parish church of Ilkley can be seen at the centre of the aerial photograph (11); its early origins are demonstrated by the Anglo-Saxon window heads shown on the previous page, and its position within the Roman fort is indicated on the simplified drawing (12).

12

Thus considerable numbers of churches seem to have been either built or adapted from existing buildings while Roman civilisation prevailed. In only a few cases is above-ground Roman fabric in a church still recognisable as such, although the number of such buildings known seems certain to increase as detailed investigations show that church after church preserves older masonry than the visible architectural features would suggest. There are sad cases when the antiquity of a fabric has only been realised too late, as at St Nicholas' church in Colchester, a heavily Victorianised edifice pulled down in 1955. Only during demolition was it realised that the church incorporated a standing Roman building.

Two West Yorkshire churches stand on or adjacent to Roman fort sites, at Ilkley and Castleford; both almost certainly have very early origins. Ilkley parish church stands within the walls of the Roman fort of Olicana (**11**, **12**); its precise relationship to the underlying Roman structures is not known, and there has only been one very limited excavation within the building. There was clearly an Anglo-Saxon stone church here; the transition from old to new religions is marked by the survival of two Anglo-Saxon window heads, each cut from a Roman altar (**10**). There is still a gap of almost five centuries between the Roman occupation of the fort and the carving of the fine Anglo-Saxon crosses now preserved in the church; the oldest part of the present church is the west wall of its nave, which might conceivably incorporate pre-Norman fabric, although the rest of the building is late medieval or Victorian.

13

Castleford church, a Victorian building on the site of its medieval predecessor, is visible towards the bottom of the aerial photograph (13). The simplified drawing (14) shows its relationship to Roman structures: it lay just outside the late 1st-century fort, on the opposite side of the Roman road and probably within a late Roman enclosure.

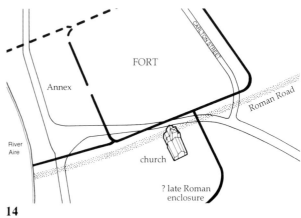

14

9

At Castleford the 'gap' in our records is even longer, but there are still tantalising hints at continuity between the Roman period and the present church. This is a typically Victorian structure of the 1860s, but its alignment, slightly north of east, conforms to that of the Roman structures in the area. The church stands just outside the west wall of the fort of Lagentium and its site may lie within a ditched annexe to the main enclosure; the east side of its churchyard abuts on the line of a Roman road (**13, 14**). The predecessor to the Victorian church was a medieval building, reputedly containing a 'Norman' arch; its much retooled font, now in the modern church at Glasshoughton, might be of 12th-century date as well.

There are other West Yorkshire churches with traces of a Roman presence. At Bardsey the massive angle quoins of the Anglo-Saxon nave and tower have lewis holes in them, a typically Roman feature, suggesting they may have been reused from a nearby building. Ledsham, probably the earliest church in the county, reuses a block with a carving of a sacrificial knife, perhaps part of a Roman altar (**9**). Finds of Roman material suggest the possible presence of a villa close to the intriguing church at Darrington, another building with evidence in its standing fabric of a pre-Norman structure.

To illuminate the survival of Christianity into the Dark Ages, after the withdrawal of the Romans, we must turn to place-name rather than archaeological evidence. At least seven place-names containing the Old English *ĕclēs*, indicative of the site of a church (e.g. Ecclesfield, near Sheffield, or Eccleshill, near Bradford), are found in the area of the 6th-century British kingdom of Elmet, into which much of what is now West Yorkshire fell. This kingdom soon succumbed to the first of the two major new groups of peoples to settle in this country between the Roman occupation and the Norman Conquest. These were Germanic tribes, Angles and Saxons, whose raiding parties harried the shores of the romanised Britain of the 4th century and who eventually settled over much of the south and east of the country. The second were the Scandinavian invaders, who first appeared on the scene with the sacking of Lindisfarne in AD 793, with consequent turmoil and upheaval lasting throughout the 8th and 9th centuries.

In the past historians have tended to suggest that each new incoming group would have 'wiped the slate clean' in the areas where they settled, eradicating previous cultural and religious traditions. Surviving documents of the period, which quite naturally have a bias towards the recording of battles and political incidents, can be used to reinforce this picture. The accumulating weight of archaeological evidence is now, however, tending to revise our view of the period, in emphasising the degree of continuity there has been in patterns of land holding and the persistence of features such as estate and field boundaries.

The 'Dark Ages' remain dark in terms of our knowledge of the survival of the Christian faith in the areas affected by the pagan Anglian settlements of the 5th and 6th centuries. Certainly the ecclesiastical systems of 200 years earlier had broken down, but that is not to say that belief and religious practices had been completely extinguished. We have the record of Augustine's mission to the south-east in AD 597, which seems to have been aimed at the conversion of the pagan English (Angles) and the reconversion of the sub-Roman British; we know that many Roman buildings remained standing and were refurbished for church use in this period.

In AD 627 Paulinus, a missionary from Rome, baptised King Edwin of Northumbria in a wooden church at York (now thought to have been built within the headquarters building of the Roman legionary fortress); after Edwin had been killed in battle against the pagan Penda his

15

16

The sculptured stone fragment above (15), showing Christ in Majesty, is from the cylindrical shaft of a massive Anglo-Saxon cross which formerly stood at Dewsbury. The drawing on the right (16) is a reconstruction by Peter Brears of the Leeds church cross shaft. The bottom panel illustrates Weland the Smith, a folk hero of the Germanic peoples of Northern Europe; it illustrates the fusion of Christian teaching with non-Christian traditions.

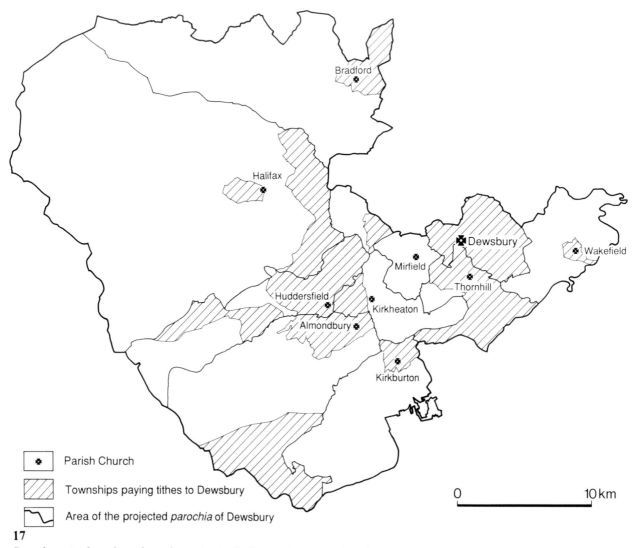

17

Dewsbury is thought to have been an Anglo-Saxon 'minster' church, centre of a large parish or parochia. *This map, drawn from* West Yorkshire: an Archaeological Survey to AD 1500, volume IV, *attempts to reconstruct the Dewsbury* parochia, *using later medieval records of tithe payments still owed to the minster by its daughter churches.*

successor Oswald invited another mission, this time from the Iona community, part of the surviving British or Celtic church. Whilst the Roman mission was aimed largely at the ruling classes, Aidan and his Celtic monks preached to the general populace. The bishopric of Lindisfarne was established in AD 635 and sent out preaching and teaching groups as far afield as Essex and the south coast, where the influence of Paulinus may have been relatively short-lived. In AD 664 the Roman and Celtic groups resolved some of their differences at the Synod of Whitby; the latter part of the century was marked by the establishment of monasteries such as the well-known joint foundation of Monkwearmouth (674) and Jarrow (681); such communities were often responsible for high-quality stone sculpture. It has been argued that the presence of 8th-century sculpture, as found at Collingham, Otley and other places in West Yorkshire, usually implies the presence of a monastery.[1]

1   As argued in E. Cambridge, 'The early church in County Durham', *Journal of the British Archaeological Association* 137 (1984), 65-85

The earliest surviving stone churches in the north of England, such as Ledsham, probably date from this period. A system of dioceses was reconstructed, many bishops' seats being established in major Roman towns which, in some fashion, had survived.

The Scandinavian invaders of the 8th century were undoubtedly savage and brutal, and saw the treasures of monasteries as a legitimate source of spoil, but once settled they seem to have been relatively tolerant of Christianity. Pagan warriors were buried in Christian churchyards, and many churches may have remained in use. Some of the smaller dioceses disappeared from the map, although that of York continued unbroken, despite a brief hiatus in AD 867, when Archbishop Wulfhere fled to Addingham in Wharfedale. Stone sculpture of the period, such as the famous Leeds crosses,[2] often mixes Christian and pagan motifs (16). There has been a great deal of debate as to the meanings of such pieces: was the carver simply 'hedging his bets'? This is the sort of question that even the most detailed archaeological investigation still leaves wide open.

By the year 900 church life was again in its ascendancy. We know far more about ecclesiastical arrangements in the Late Saxon period than at earlier times. It would appear that four classes of churches were recognised: the head minster or cathedral which was the seat of a bishop, the lesser minster or mother church, the parish church, and the field chapel. In West Yorkshire, parishes are usually made up of several townships, the township being the earliest and most basic unit in the historic landscape, possibly having its origin in Romano-British estates. The lowest status group of field chapels or *feldcircan* is somewhat shadowy; they were differentiated from parish churches by not having their own graveyards, and were probably mostly private foundations.

Some elements of this four-fold hierarchy were to persist for 1000 years. A local example is seen in the annual pensions paid to the vicarage of Dewsbury from the parishes of Almondbury, Bradford, Huddersfield, Kirkburton, Kirkheaton and Thornhill, amongst others; despite being a source of dispute in the Commonwealth period, these were still being paid in the 19th century.[3] The explanation of all this seems to be that Dewsbury was a lesser minster or mother church, and that the individual parishes had been carved out of its territory before the Norman Conquest (17).[4]

Many of the parishes in the western part of the county were divided into chapelries. There is little documentary evidence for the origins of these; often the earliest written records are of 15th or 16th-century date. It seems possible that they have their origins in Anglo-Saxon field chapels. Chapelries such as Heptonstall, Horbury and Tong appear to have had substantial early medieval buildings, comparable in size to some contemporary parish churches; excavation is our best hope of determining their date of foundation.

So far we have been looking at churches as buildings. Remains of pre-Conquest fabric have now been recognised in a number of West Yorkshire churches, but in many more, Anglo-Saxon or Anglo-Scandinavian evidence is seen in sculptured stones, sometimes grave slabs but more usually carved free-standing crosses (15). There is still some doubt as to what these signified. The 9th-century *Life of St Willibald* states that the estates of many English lords at that time had no

---

2   See A. McGuire and A. Clark, *The Leeds Crosses* (1987, Museum of Leeds)

3   See S.J. Chadwick, 'Notes on Dewsbury church and some of its rectors and vicars', *Yorkshire Archaeological Journal* 20 (1909), 369-446

4   Another example of an Anglo-Saxon minster is Kippax, which seems to have covered the later parishes of Swillington, Garforth and Whitkirk (information from R.E. Yarwood).

church, only 'a cross raised on high where daily prayers were said'. Other sources speak of 'preaching crosses', and crosses were also raised to commemorate events; for example there is an old tradition of a cross at Dewsbury with an inscription referring to Paulinus preaching there in AD 627. They were also used to mark burials. The majority of early cross remains in West Yorkshire are in parish churches, but there are a few examples, such as the Walton Cross (of which only the massive base remains) and the crosses of which fragments have been found at East Riddlesden and Stansfield, which may always have stood alone.

A final view of the Anglo-Saxon period is given in the Domesday Book, compiled for William the Conqueror in 1086. This includes references to 23 churches in what is now West Yorkshire; there were clearly others (Ledsham for instance is not mentioned), and the reason for the selection is not clear. It is however reasonable to assume that the Domesday references confirm the existence of pre-Norman churches; foundations between the Conquest and 1086 would be highly unlikely. Taken together, the evidence of standing buildings, stone sculpture and the Domesday references shows that by the Late Saxon period there were churches in at least 42 of the 55 medieval parishes within the present county, sufficient to indicate that a system of local churches was already well established.

18
Original doorway and window in the south wall of the Anglo-Saxon west porch (now the base of the tower) at Ledsham; the decorative carving on the doorway is the result of Victorian restoration, but it may copy what was there before.

CHAPTER THREE

The Anglo-Saxon Churches

Turning to the church buildings themselves, West Yorkshire has three which have long been recognised as of Anglo-Saxon date. Ledsham is the best preserved and almost certainly the earliest; it includes the nave walls, west porch and south *porticus* of a building which may well date from around AD 700. Quite a number of features – the plan of the nave with an early west porch, the form of the masonry, and the construction of the windows – all show similarities to those of 'early' churches in Northumberland and Durham (in particular St Peter's church at Monkwearmouth, erected by Benedict Biscop in 674). The west porch has an original doorway on the south, but the carving of the vine scroll ornament on its stripwork surround dates only from the 1871 restoration carried out by the architect Henry Curzon; there has been considerable debate as to whether his carving reproduced an older feature or simply 'improved' a plain piece of stonework (**18**).[1] The porch originally had two storeys; two original windows, one above the other, survive on the south, and the upper room also has a window opening into the nave. Such an upper room at the west end is a feature of several important Anglo-Saxon churches, such as Deerhurst in Gloucestershire and Brixworth in Northamptonshire; it has been suggested that the local lord or magnate would sit here to observe the service taking place in the church below. In the Late Saxon or early Norman period the porch was converted into a tower; the present belfry, built of neatly squared white magnesian limestone in contrast to the rubble of the 'middle stage', is clearly 12th century (**19, 20**).

The simple round-headed Anglo-Saxon chancel arch survives intact; here the only carved ornament is a band of four-petalled flower-like motifs on the imposts; once again much of the carving only dates from Curzon's restoration, but enough of the original survives to show that in this case at least he was following the correct pattern. Professor Richard Bailey has recently pointed out parallels to this design in Continental art, and has suggested that it 'fits most comfortably into a 7th or early 8th-century context'.[2] The nave also retains remains of several original windows, now blocked up, in its side walls. These, like the tower windows, have external arched heads cut from a single stone (like those fashioned from the Roman altars at Ilkley), and round-headed rear arches. In each wall two windows were set on either side of a central *porticus*.

---

1 See L.A.S. Butler, 'Ledsham church: the south doorway of the tower', *Journal of the British Archaeological Association* 140 (1987), 199-203; and M.L. Faull, 'The decoration of the south doorway of Ledsham church tower', *Journal of the British Archaeological Association* 139 (1986), 143-47

2 R.N. Bailey, 'Ledsham', *Bulletin of the Council for British Archaeology Churches Committee* 18 (1983), 6-8

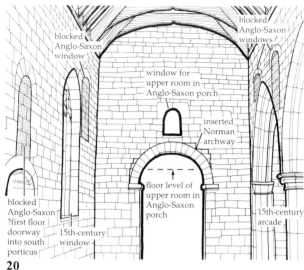

19 **20**

The photograph (19) and key drawing (20) of the west end of Ledsham nave show the remaining Anglo-Saxon features (windows and porticus *doorway) and later insertions (tower arch, arcade and large window).*

The term '*porticus*' (Latin for porch) is now generally used for the chambers which are sometimes found flanking the main body of an Anglo-Saxon church; what function these fulfilled is still something of a mystery. Many contained altars, and burials were often made within them, but they may have had other uses as well. At Ledsham the northern *porticus* has been swept away by the addition of the 15th-century north aisle, but the southern one has survived, although cut down in height and converted into the medieval south porch. It is noticeable that this porch is set unusually far east in comparison with other medieval south porches, which tend to be closer to the west end of the nave. Above the present south door, which looks 18th century, is a tall blocked opening with a round arch towards the nave. Is this the upper part of an abnormally tall and narrow doorway, or is it an opening into a first-floor chamber within the *porticus*? Anglo-Saxon churches often possessed high-level chambers, in all parts of the building; these might have housed further altars, or provided accommodation for priests.

A second church long recognised as preserving Anglo-Saxon fabric is Bardsey, between Leeds and Wetherby. Here the most striking feature is the tall and narrow west tower with its double belfry windows of a characteristic Late Saxon type. The nave walls are Anglo-Saxon as well, but here both are pierced by medieval arcades; their only original features, besides the massive western angle quoins, are the remains of two windows in the north wall. These, since most of their dressed stone surrounds were removed before they were blocked, show as little more than round-headed areas of rubble patching (**21, 22**). The tower at Bardsey is usually interpreted as having been raised on an earlier porch (as at Ledsham, Monkwearmouth and elsewhere), but it possesses several features which are not yet fully understood. Compared with other pre-Conquest towers, one rather surprising feature at Bardsey is that there seems to be no visible evidence of a doorway into a gallery or upper chamber over the nave. The west ends of the Norman aisles overlap the tower, and may incorporate walling of Anglo-Saxon *porticus*.

St Oswald's church at Collingham, quite close to Bardsey, has Anglo-Saxon fabric in its nave walls, recognisable by the heavy side-alternate angle quoins. Contemporary work may also survive in the western part of the chancel (extended to the east in the medieval period); only fragmentary

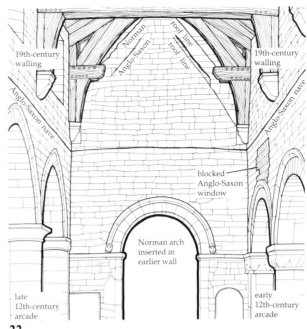

21   **22**

The west end of Bardsey church is, like Ledsham, largely an Anglo-Saxon structure with later insertions (principally the tower arch and arcades). The photograph (21) and key drawing (22) show the original roof line and blocked Anglo-Saxon windows.

remains of architectural features can be traced today. Collingham church was heavily 'gothicised', after the fashion of the day, in 1840-41; Joseph Morris described it as 'wretchedly restored at some dark period'.[3] Many features of interest were probably destroyed or concealed, but one good result was the discovery of two 9th-century crosses, one with an inscription showing that it is a funerary monument.

As a result of the recent survey, Saxon fabric can now be shown to survive (or its survival may be inferred with varying degrees of probability) in a considerable number of other West Yorkshire churches. One of the clearest cases is at Bramham, only about 5km south-east of Collingham. The siting of this church in a huge oval churchyard (**23**), unique in the county, is enough to arouse suspicions that the building, or at least its site, is of relatively early date; the recent discovery of an Anglo-Scandinavian bone pin in the churchyard backs this up. Until recently the church had been seen as another rather over-restored medieval building, its earliest portions a mid-12th-century west tower and north arcade. The nave walls above the arcades, concealed by plaster inside and by refacing outside, are surprisingly thin (0.60-0.65m) for a Norman church; evidence for a Saxon date is confirmed by the north-west angle quoin of the nave, which is of a massive side-alternate type. The reason that this seems to have escaped previous attention is that it can be seen only from inside the Victorian stair turret built in the angle between the tower and the west end of the north aisle. There are some similarly massive gritstone quoins, clearly reused, at the east end of the 13th-century chancel.

Dewsbury parish church is another case where the evidence of early angle quoins has been overlooked in the past. Considering the historical evidence for the town being the site of a Saxon

3   J.E. Morris, *Little Guide to the West Riding of Yorkshire* (1923, 2nd ed.), 154

minster church (its dependent chapelries resulted in a medieval parish covering over 400 square miles), the ancient tradition that Paulinus preached here in 627, and the important collection of Anglo-Saxon sculpture in the church, this oversight is all the more surprising. The church has been so heavily altered that its external elevations are all of 18th and 19th-century date; inside only the nave walls survive from the medieval building. These are pierced by rather fine 13th-century arcades; standing in the north aisle one can see, just east of the easternmost pillar of the north arcade, one massive block of an original north-east quoin, with three smaller blocks above. One corner of the largest block has been cut off by the inserted 13th-century arch (**24, 25**). On the opposite face of the wall, towards the nave, an irregular patch of masonry shows the position of the cut-away east wall to which the quoins belonged. There is similar evidence, although not quite so clear, in the south wall. The remains are admittedly fragmentary, but are sufficient to show that at one stage Dewsbury church had a nave 15.00 by 5.60m (internally) with walls 0.67m (north) and 0.70-0.76m (south) thick, constructed of rubble fabric with megalithic angle quoins. This nave was extended eastwards before the present arcades were inserted. In view of both the historical and sculptural evidence, and the fabric and quoin types of the nave walls, there seem good grounds for believing that the bare skeleton of the nave of Dewsbury's Anglo-Saxon minster still survives.

Domesday Book, compiled in 1086, refers to two churches within the manor of Wakefield. One of these was probably the present Wakefield Cathedral; the other may have been St Helen's church at Sandal Magna, on the southern outskirts of Wakefield. Sandal Magna church has a

23
Circular or oval churchyards are regarded as indications of early, possibly Celtic, Christian sites. The large oval churchyard at Bramham is clearly visible in this aerial photograph.

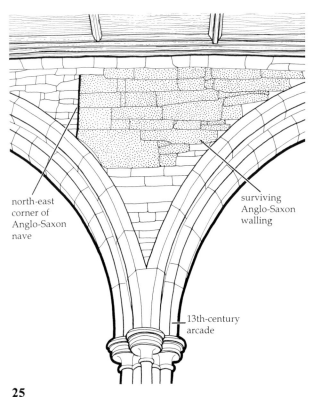

24   **25**

*Anglo-Saxon walling has now been recognised in Dewsbury church. The photograph (**24**) shows, above the later arcade, what appears to be the east end of the original nave wall; the early masonry is shaded on the key drawing (**25**).*

cruciform plan, with a central tower, a six-bay aisled nave (the western two bays are an extension of 1872), transepts, and a chancel with a south chapel. This type of plan is in itself a rarity in West Yorkshire: it occurs today only at Crofton and at All Saints, Pontefract, though the traditional interpretation of Wakefield Cathedral implies that this was cruciform at one stage; in addition, the demolished medieval churches at Castleford and Leeds were of this type. Sandal Magna is usually thought of as a mid-12th-century church thoroughly remodelled in the 14th century; looking again at the 'mid-12th-century' parts – the lower parts of the crossing, and some walling in the transepts – they in fact possess several features that hint at pre-Conquest traditions. There are three main pieces of evidence. First, in plan the central square of the crossing has salient angles which project into the nave aisles (**27**).[4] This is held to be a distinctively Anglo-Saxon feature, exemplified by the well-preserved Anglo-Saxon church at Stow, north of Lincoln, and also at Norton on Teesside, as well as by several Anglo-Saxon churches in the south of England. Secondly, the west wall of the south transept retains a short length of a string-course of plain square section, another feature unusual after the Norman Conquest. Thirdly, the quite elaborate mouldings of the responds to the crossing arches, and their bases (**26**), have no local parallels, and are quite different from authentic 12th-century work in the area. Unfortunately both the 14th-century remodelling, and the replacement and retooling of much of the stonework during the 19th-century restoration combine to obscure original detail; the only unaltered pre-14th-century features seem to be the respond bases with their strange channelled corners. The Sandal crossing in its original form seems to be more Anglo-Saxon

---

4   These can be seen to the west; later alterations have masked the eastern corners.

than Norman in style, but its actual date remains uncertain; all that can be safely said is that St Helen's was already a relatively large and elaborate building by *c.* 1100.

It is well known that the use of the Anglo-Saxon style persisted after the Norman Conquest, producing what is termed the 'Saxo-Norman overlap'. Several churches in South Yorkshire show features transitional between the two styles, or features of both which can be shown by other evidence to be contemporary with each other; these buildings are usually ascribed to the late 11th or early 12th century. A West Yorkshire church that may belong to the 'overlap' period is at Guiseley. Here the Norman south arcade, probably of mid-12th-century date, is cut through an earlier wall which has three megalithic blocks at the base of its south-east angle quoin. These are certainly more Anglo-Saxon than Norman in appearance, but at the foot of the wall is a chamfered plinth, which would be unusual before the Conquest; cases are known, however, of plinths being inserted into the foot of an earlier wall. The thickness of the wall, between 0.80 and 0.85m, is not distinctive one way or the other (Norman walls tend to be 0.90 to 1.00m thick; Anglo-Saxon 0.60 to 0.70m), nor are the remains of a blocked window (its head missing) above the arcade. Changes in masonry in both nave walls hint that there was an extension to the east before either arcade (the northern one is 15th century) was pierced through. Guiseley demonstrates the problems of ascertaining the date of fabric which lacks distinctive architectural features; evidence for an Anglo-Saxon origin is, however, strengthened by the presence of a 9th-century cross shaft in the church, and by a stone above the south arcade (frustratingly obscured by mortar) which may be an early monolithic window head.

Even more confusing is the delightful church at Darrington near Pontefract. Here the nave is tall and relatively narrow, with walls 0.76m thick; a fragment of a square-section string-course at the south-west corner strengthens the case for the survival of Anglo-Saxon fabric although, as at Bramham, plaster within and refacing without make it difficult to absolutely certain. As at Bardsey, the nave aisles extend to embrace the west tower: this in itself has been cited as a clue to an Anglo-

26

*Two unusual and probably early features of Sandal Magna church are the channelled bases of the responds (**26**) and the salient angles of the central square of the crossing (**27**).*

27

28
The patchwork of differing stone types in the tower at Darrington; the sandstone parts may represent an original pre-Conquest structure.

Saxon building, on the grounds that it results from *porticus* flanking the tower being incorporated in later aisles. The tower at Darrington is one of the most puzzling in the county (**28**). It is constructed of a bewildering variety of stone types including squared rubble in which limestone and sandstone are mixed, sandstone, and well-squared limestone blocks of various sizes. The west wall looks as if it has collapsed and been rebuilt at some time, but on the north, above the aisle roof, is an area of roughly shaped sandstone blocks. Above this the belfry is of well-squared limestone. The sandstone appears to be stratigraphically older than the limestone; all the features associated with the limestone parts of the tower seem to be of 12th-century date. This discrepancy in stone type is seen again at Laughton-en-le-Morthen in South Yorkshire where the pre-Conquest part of the church is of red sandstone (imported from some distance away), whilst the 12th-century parts are of local magnesian limestone. The same situation again seems to occur at Aycliffe in Durham, where the Anglo-Saxon parts of a church which now stands right on the edge of a magnesian limestone quarry are of imported sandstone. All this points to the unwillingness of at least some Anglo-Saxon builders to use the relatively soft limestone. Inside the tower at Darrington are more features which strongly suggest that its lower parts are of Anglo-Saxon date: the nave string-course is continued to link up with some unusual stripwork on the south side of the tower (which is unfortunately partly hidden by the aisle roof), and the tower arch itself is of Anglo-Saxon proportions and uses the Anglo-Saxon technique of having 'through stones', voussoirs which extend the whole thickness of the wall, although sadly almost the whole arch, in its present form, is the product of an 1880 restoration.

There is another group of churches in which evidence for Anglo-Saxon work is much more tenuous, but cannot be discounted. Two of these are in the valley of the Wharfe, and have important pre-Conquest associations with the archbishops of York. Addingham (**29**), where Wulfhere fled in 867, stands within an Iron Age ditched enclosure overlooking the south bank of the river, and is clearly on a defensible site. There is part of an Anglo-Saxon cross inside the church,[5] and an Anglo-Saxon comb case was found in the sealing level of the Iron Age ditch in 1972. A group of burials excavated on the west side of the churchyard in 1990 proved to be of Anglo-Saxon date. The church is at first sight an attractive Georgian building, dated 1757, but closer examination reveals that this is in fact a recasing of a medieval structure, the late medieval north arcade and north aisle of which survive intact, as well as the rather fine nave roof. Internally the walls are concealed by plaster, but there is a curious feature at the north-east corner of the nave, now within the aisle which extends into a chancel chapel. The corner has been cut back, perhaps to allow a view of the altar from the aisle (a not uncommon practice), but the cutting back is very irregular, as if the workmen responsible had had to struggle with difficult material – perhaps the megalithic blocks of an Anglo-Saxon quoin?

Otley is an even more tantalising case, and perhaps the most exciting possibility of all. An important collection of early sculpture strongly suggests that there was a monastery here in the 9th century; not far from the church was a palace of the archbishops of York, who had major estates here from an early date. The palace possessed its own chapel, excavated a few years ago; this was, in its earliest phase, a large apsidal-ended structure which may have been pre-Conquest in its earliest phase.[6] All Saints church has a number of very puzzling features. Chief among these is the size of

---

5   Other pieces of early sculpture were found in the tower walls in about 1984, but have been plastered over again.

6   H.E.J. Le Patourel and P. Wood, 'Excavation of the Archbishop of York's Manor House at Otley', *Yorkshire Archaeological Journal* 45 (1973), 115-41

29

Addingham was a refuge for Archbishop Wulfhere of York in 867, and would almost certainly have contained a church at that time. Excavations by the Archaeology Service in 1990-91 uncovered burials dated to the 8th and 9th centuries.

its nave, which is both long (26.50m) and extremely wide (9m). These dimensions have no parallel in any other early medieval church in the county. Plaster conceals the walls internally, and externally there has been much refacing. At the north-west corner, however, a few quoin stones are visible; the coursed stones of the 14th-century refacing, coeval with the present west tower, are cut to fit round them. Neither the size of the quoins nor the thickness of the nave walls (0.80-0.85m) is distinctive enough to endorse a date one side of the Conquest or the other. The chancel, which is of 12th-century date and generally held to be the oldest part of the church, has angle quoins of quite different type. As a general rule in the medieval development of a church the nave walls tend to be retained when the nave is enlarged by the addition of aisles or transepts, whilst the chancel tends to be extended eastwards or completely rebuilt. Otley has both aisles and transepts, but these have been added on to a nave which was already of quite extraordinary dimensions; the north aisle, which has a Norman door, probably reset, looks to be of more than one build, as if it might have replaced, stage by stage, a series of *porticus*. If the chancel at Otley is later than the nave, then it would seem quite likely that the nave is of Anglo-Saxon date. If this is the case, it is unquestionably the largest surviving Anglo-Saxon structure in the north of England, and must represent a major monastic or minster church. Unfortunately not enough evidence is exposed today to prove or disprove this hypothesis; the church was roughly handled by the Victorians, when the lowering of floor levels may have destroyed much of the sub-floor archaeology. To date the mystery remains unsolved.

23

Another church which was already a large and elaborate structure by a relatively early medieval date was Kirkburton. As this stands today it is basically a 13th-century building with a six-bay aisled nave, a west tower, and a long chancel. The nave provides remains of an earlier south-east quoin, yet its walls are not as thick as one would expect in a 12th-century building, and the church contains a Late Saxon (?11th century) cross. It is a building that needs further careful study. Other churches similarly have masonry in their nave walls that pre-dates their earliest architectural features, and which might conceivably be pre-Conquest. Normanton, South Kirkby and perhaps Almondbury fall into this category.

In addition to structural remains, a considerable number of West Yorkshire churches possess pre-Conquest sculpture (see Chapter Two); the collection of stones from Kirkheaton, now in the Tolson Memorial Museum in Huddersfield, includes a decorated monolithic window head that seems clearly Anglo-Saxon (31), showing that there was a stone church on this site before the Norman Conquest.

Before leaving the subject of Anglo-Saxon churches, it is interesting to note the dedications of the buildings containing, or thought to contain, early fabric. Sixteen churches are referred to above as possessing either proven or suspected pre-Conquest or 'overlap' fabric, or as standing on known Roman sites; this is out of a total of 69 medieval churches and chapels covered by the survey. These sixteen include no less than twelve of the 21 All Saints or All Hallows dedications. Of the other four churches in the group, two are dedicated to St Oswald (Collingham and Guiseley), one to St Helen (Sandal Magna) and one to St Peter (Addingham). Of the other nine All Saints dedications, five possess pre-Conquest sculpture and a sixth (Pontefract) is a cruciform church, possibly of early origins, with a small Anglo-Saxon church recently discovered by excavation just outside its churchyard (30). The correlation between All Saints or All Hallows dedications and early churches or sculpture would seem, in this area at least, to have been established as a significant one.

30

31

The pre-Conquest church excavated by the Archaeology Service at Tanner's Row, Pontefract (30) consisted of a small nave (top) and chancel (bottom; east end destroyed). The window head from Kirkheaton (31) would have come from a similar building.

CHAPTER FOUR

The Impact of the Normans

The coming of the Normans brought a renewed vigour to church building throughout England, which in part may have sprung from a conscious desire to assert themselves and stamp a Norman presence on an Anglo-Saxon landscape. The great churches they built – the cathedrals and those serving monastic houses – outdid in scale anything that had gone before, and their style too was vividly different with a love of geometrical patterns and a variety of distinctive ornaments. As with any change in culture, new architectural forms and modes of construction spread from centres of influence such as the new monasteries; the village churches round about would relatively soon reflect the coming of the new style whilst in those further away their influence would be felt more slowly. As already mentioned there is a hybrid style called the 'Saxo-Norman overlap'. This is most likely to be found in churches which were away from the main roads, and which were distant from the new abbeys and priories of the late 11th and early 12th centuries. Despite all this new building and social change, one can still occasionally identify a few backwaters where the Norman style seems never to have arrived; here the stylistic overlap is not between the Anglo-Saxon and the Norman, but between the dimly remembered Anglo-Saxon and the incoming Gothic, a century and a half after the Battle of Hastings.

Despite the presence of several major monasteries, such as the Cluniac priory at Pontefract (founded *c.* 1090), the Augustinian priory at Nostell (founded *c.* 1114) and the Cistercian abbey of Kirkstall (founded 1152), West Yorkshire is not a great county for Norman architecture, although it does possess one church, Adel, which must rate as of national significance.

Probably the earliest recognisable group of Norman churches in the area are those characterised by their use of herringbone fabric. There are a number of these around York, and others further south, usually on or near the Magnesian Limestone escarpment. Herringbone is a very distinctive type of construction in which small pieces of stone (typically fragments of thinly bedded limestone) are laid diagonally, so that pieces of dissimilar thickness can nonetheless be used to produce a course of even height. In the past the dating of this fabric type has aroused much controversy; in the 19th century it was thought to be proof of Anglo-Saxon date, but Professor Baldwin Brown argued the contrary,[1] that it was an indicant of Norman work. More recent studies show that herringbone fabric has been used at various times in the past; it has been found in Roman buildings, in known Anglo-Saxon churches, in Norman buildings and even in 18th and 19th-century

---

1   G. Baldwin Brown, *The Arts in Early England* Vol. II (1903, reprinted 1925)

farm buildings (e.g. in Holderness, Humberside). Constraints for its use seem to be predominantly the economics of a difficult building material, although in some cases its decorative effect may have played a part as well.

The West Yorkshire churches characterised by their herringbone work are probably mostly of the late 11th and early 12th centuries, although a few could be earlier; in Farndon in Nottinghamshire herringbone fabric occurs along with a distinctly pre-Conquest doorway in a surviving *porticus*. Kippax is probably the most dramatic example of the Yorkshire group, a church of simple plan – aisleless nave, west tower and chancel – but of substantial size, standing on a hilltop close to the earthworks of a castle (probably wooden) of *c*. 1100 (**32**). The original windows were small and round-headed, and in the Anglo-Saxon tradition of being set high in the wall; there was a pair of opposed doorways towards the west end of the nave. Whilst the shell of the church remains intact, it seems to have suffered a severe fire around 1300 which badly damaged the dressed stonework, the windows and doorways all having to be replaced. The original tower arch remains, but is so decayed as to show little of its form and nothing of its detail.

32

33

34

*Examples of early Norman herringbone masonry at Kippax (**32**), Aberford (**33**; during demolition) and Felkirk (**34**).*

26

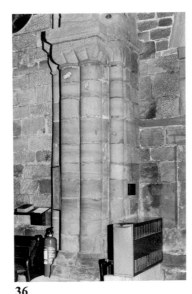

The megalithic blocks of an earlier (?Norman) respond can be seen behind a 15th-century respond at Barwick (35); the highly decorated responds of Felkirk tower arch (36) probably came originally from a chancel archway of c. 1100.

35　　　　　　　　　　　　36

Barwick in Elmet is another member of the group, but has suffered more alteration than Kippax. The chancel still shows much herringbone work, but only one original window (now opening into the vestry) survives. Later medieval aisles have been added to the nave, where the original fabric survives only at the four corners. Although the nave is usually thought to have been aisleless in its original form, the eastern responds of the 15th-century arcades seem to be built up against earlier responds composed, like the eastern nave quoins, of megalithic blocks of almost Anglo-Saxon appearance (35). The western responds of the arcades, in contrast, are set against roughly cut stubs of rubble walling. This may imply that the original church possessed transepts or side chapels; another possibility is that the church may have been built in the pre-Conquest tradition, with *porticus*.

Herringbone masonry appears in the much more fragmentary remains of the early Norman nave at Felkirk (34). The spectacular feature here is the carved architectural detail, notably absent at Kippax and Barwick; here gritstone rather than limestone is the local building material. The responds of the present tower arch are probably those of a chancel arch of *c.* 1100, reset; their scalloped capitals have cable moulding and a variety of ornament including intersecting round arches, star ornament, incised knots and a row of human heads (36). Several of the motifs, including the heads, are reminiscent of the elaborate font now in the late 19th-century church at Skelmanthorpe, formerly belonging to High Hoyland church just over the border into South Yorkshire. A lot more carved stones, presumably from the same arch, have been reused in the internal walls of the tower; these include voussoirs with chevron moulding and longer stones, presumably from the hoodmould, with billet moulding and sunk star ornament. In the south aisle wall is a reused megalithic window head with incised lines concentric to the arch; on its own it would be easy to see this as an Anglo-Saxon piece, but in the context of the other reused material at Felkirk it is almost certainly part of the same church as the reset arch responds and the herringbone masonry. Old photographs taken during the 1861 rebuilding show that Aberford church formerly had herringbone work in its nave (33); one window which survives, reset in the Victorian chancel, has a monolithic arched head of Anglo-Saxon type, but it is stamped as post-Conquest by its chamfered hoodmould.

37

38

39

40

41

The finest Norman church in West Yorkshire is Adel, which contains a highly decorated chancel arch (37) with capitals depicting the Baptism of Christ and the Descent from the Cross (38; 39). Outside, the corbel table is formed by a series of grotesque human and animal heads (40), and the door ring has the head of a monster devouring a man (41).

42   43

*The Norman belfry openings at Bramham (**42***) and Ledsham (**43***) are closely comparable in design.*

As already mentioned, West Yorkshire has one very important Norman church, that of St John the Baptist at Adel. Its construction has been linked with a charter of *c.* 1140, although most architectural historians have placed it around 1150-60. Adel church appears to be a building all of one period and is, like Kippax, of a very simple plan, in this case only a nave and chancel, but quite large. The building material is gritstone, and the cut dressings have weathered relatively well. The south door has been called 'perhaps the finest and best known of the Yorkshire Norman doorways':[2] it is of five orders moulded with beakheads, rolls and zig-zag in various forms. The imposts have capitals carved with animals, birds, foliage and strapwork. The arch is set in a shallow porch-like projection or door case, the gable of which is filled with sculptured panels – at the apex an *Agnus Dei*, with, below, Christ in Majesty flanked by the symbols of the Evangelists; these are above more worn designs which have been identified as the golden candlestick and the tree of life (**47**). After this spectacular display the rest of the exterior is relatively plain, with a plinth and moulded string below small round-headed windows which are set between pilaster buttresses; only at the wall head does the Norman love of intricate sculpture break loose again in a corbel table with a series of grotesque human and animal heads (**40**). A few corbels have busts, presumably of saints, under round-arched recesses, harking back to those on one of the 8th-century crosses at Otley.

Inside Adel church the most striking feature is the chancel arch (**37**); here the carvings are surprisingly fresh. There are three orders towards the nave with zig-zag, radial and concentric rolls linked to produce what Pevsner calls 'a chain of box frames',[3] and a series of grotesque masks.

2   C.E. Keyser, 'The Norman doorways of Yorkshire', *Memorials of Old Yorkshire* (1909; ed. T. M. Fallow), 183

3   N. Pevsner, *Buildings of England: Yorkshire The West Riding* (1967, 2nd ed.), 339

*The three surviving Norman arcades in West Yorkshire, at Bardsey (**44**), Guiseley (**45**) and Bramham (**46**), range in date from the early to the late 12th century.*

44

Some are similar to those on the corbel table outside; their identification and significance have tested the imagination of generations of antiquarians and historians. On the chancel arch capitals the Baptism of Christ (**38**) and Descent from the Cross (**39**) are more readily identified; there are also a centaur with a bow, a horseman in 12th-century armour, and various beasts.

The elaboration of carved detail at a church like Adel is clearly the product of a wealthy patron, whereas other churches of the period were much plainer. The chapel at Lotherton Hall lies at the opposite end of the scale. Like Adel it has a simple two-cell plan, but it is built of rubble, and its architectural features are much simpler. The chancel arch seems to have been removed during 18th-century alterations; the north door has a moulded arch of two orders, the outer carried on capitals with simple leaf ornament pointing to a relatively late Norman date, perhaps *c.* 1170. The south door has an absolutely plain round arch; two of the three original windows have minimal decoration to their heads, in the form of radial incised lines.

No other Norman church in the county remains in anything like its original form. Three churches on the Magnesian Limestone, Aberford, Bramham and Ledsham, have west towers with 12th-century belfries of a very similar form, the belfry openings having twin round-arched lights enclosed within a larger arch (**42, 43**). Darrington is another church on the limestone where the belfry seems 12th century; its paired openings lack the enclosing arch, and may be a Norman copy of the Anglo-Saxon paired openings seen at churches like Bardsey. Birstall has the lower part of a Norman tower (much restored) but its belfry is 15th century; in other parts of Yorkshire there are sufficient numbers of 12th-century towers which lack original upper stages to prompt the suggestion that they originally carried timber belfries. The lower part of the tower at Batley also shows quite small well-squared stonework which looks of 12th-century date, but it has lost all its original architectural features.

One major difference between the churches of the Anglo-Saxon period and those of the 12th and 13th centuries lies in the way that the interior of the building is divided up. Anglo-Saxon

45

46

churches tended to be divided into a series of separate compartments: tower and chancel arches might be closed by doors, and the *porticus* flanking the main body of the building were each a separate chamber. After the Norman Conquest ranges of *porticus* were replaced by aisles, opening to the body of the church by means of a continuous arcade rather than a series of doorways. Although there are one or two Late Saxon examples, aisles are very much a Norman innovation. At parish church level, 12th- century aisles were usually very narrow; their initial function seems to have been to provide a passageway round the building to be used in processions. Making such an aisle involved the construction of an open row or arcade of arches between the two parts of the building. If an aisle was being added to an older nave, this was usually done by building the arches and piers into the wall, and removing the masonry beneath when this work was complete. Only occasionally (and if for instance a wall was unduly thick and would be too heavy for the arcade to carry) did the builders take down the wall and start again from ground level, with all the use of scaffolding and centering that this entailed.

Only three Norman arcades survive in West Yorkshire: on the north side of the naves at Bardsey (**44**) and Bramham (**46**), and on the south at Guiseley (**45**); all are cut through earlier walls. The Bardsey arcade is probably the earliest, and has been dated to *c.* 1100-1125. It has heavy round piers with scalloped capitals carrying round arches of one square order, with a hoodmould which, like that of the tower arch (inserted into the Anglo-Saxon tower at around the same time that the arcade was constructed), is ornamented with a groove, and a chamfer to its lower angle. The Guiseley arcade is rather more elaborate; the piers, still massive, are of quatrefoil plan (the earliest members of a stylistic tradition that extends through at least two centuries) and have scalloped capitals except for the central one, which has a capital with rudimentary leaf ornament. The arches themselves are of two square orders rather than one; this may be because the wall through which the arcade is cut is rather thicker than at Bardsey.

47

49

50

48

51

A series of Norman doorways: Adel (47), Bardsey (48), East Ardsley (49), Guiseley (50) and Otley (51), the last two showing the changes in style in the later 12th century.

52   53

Two Norman tympana: the reconstruction drawing of the Emley example (52) shows the Lion of Judah and the Agnus Dei; *the latter reappears on the more complete Woolley tympanum (53).*

The arcade at Bramham is quite different in its proportions from the other two, so much so as to prompt a suspicion that it has been interfered with in the 'gallery era' of the 18th century. The three arches are still of one plain square order (as at Bardsey they are cut through a relatively thin Anglo-Saxon wall) but they are tall and broad, on lofty round piers with the simplest of square capitals; the bases have rather more elaborate mouldings, suggesting that they belong to the later 12th century and the 'Transitional' style, the overlap between 'Romanesque' (both Anglo-Saxon and Norman) and Gothic. The Bramham arcade is probably one of the latest in the area to use the round or semicircular arch, the hallmark of the Romanesque styles.

Apart from the occasional arcade, the principal surviving features of Norman churches are the two that provide an opportunity for the display of decorative carving: the south door and the chancel arch. Doorways of the 12th century, usually on the south of the nave but occasionally elsewhere, are especially interesting, both as architectural features in themselves and in the way that they have been treated by subsequent builders.

The doorways are a showcase for the range of decorative mouldings that are familiar subjects in architectural textbooks. Adel (**47**) is by far the most elaborate, but there are other examples in the parish churches of Bardsey (**48**), East Ardsley (**49**), Guiseley (**50**), Hartshead, Otley (**51**), and Thorp Arch, as well as some remains at both Kippax and Kirkthorpe; in addition there is a Norman doorway of sorts in the vestry at Beeston (Leeds) but this is simply made up of various 12th-century architectural fragments discovered in a 19th-century rebuilding. The Bardsey door is probably of the same date as the north arcade. It has chevron moulding and beakheads in the arch; the outer orders rest on jamb shafts with scalloped capitals which show the same sunk semicircular panels as the tower arch respond capitals at Felkirk.

The sunk panels, a little more elaborate in form and edged with a beaded moulding, are seen again on the capitals at Thorp Arch, where the outer order of the arch is made up of a fine set of fifteen beakheads, all varying in detail. None of the West Yorkshire doorways has an *in situ* tympanum (the panel between the square head of the door itself and the arch). At Thorp Arch, however, a broken tympanum, probably from the present doorway, is built into the wall of the porch; it bears a simple chequer-board pattern. Emley (**52**) and Woolley (**53**) both have reset tympana, the former (over a piscina) with two beasts and the latter (over the door to the rood loft stair) with the *Agnus Dei.*

Chip-carved panels (seen on the reused voussoirs at Felkirk) decorate the capitals of the doorway at East Ardsley, which has an arch with raised saltire crosses on the inner order and chevron

33

on the two outer; on the outermost order the chevron is interrupted by two beakheads at the apex. The hoodmould again displays a variety of pattern types, showing that the 12th-century masons were not unduly concerned with symmetry. A similar range of motifs appears on the Hartshead doorway (**55**), with some additions such as the band of zig-zag with pellets which runs along the abaci. The Guiseley doorway is probably 20 or 30 years later, and a real change in form and feeling has taken place. The arch is still round, but in its capitals the scalloping and panel decoration has given way to various leaf forms, and in the arch the sharp geometry of chevron and grotesque zoomorphic forms of beakheads has been displaced by a simple roll moulding between two chamfers. The last in the sequence of Norman doorways (if one can draw a distinction between 'Norman' and 'Transitional') is Otley, where the leaf forms of the capitals are both simpler and more elegant, and the arch has a plain and narrow chamfer.

Of all the Norman doorways in West Yorkshire churches, only those at Adel and Lotherton Hall can definitely be said to be in their original positions. Most of the others have been dismantled and re-erected when aisles were added or widened, or churches rebuilt. What is especially interesting is that this did not just happen in the 19th century, when interest in church architecture had been awakened, but that it happened, all over the country, in the medieval period. The Bardsey and Otley doorways, and probably those at Guiseley and Hartshead as well (where 19th-century rebuilding has obscured the evidence), were reset in the later medieval period. The Thorp Arch doorway has been moved at least twice: it is now conventionally sited in the nave south wall, but prior to 1872 it was in the west wall of the 15th-century tower. The frequent medieval reuse of doorways seems to be something more than a utilitarian resiting of features for the sake of economy (although this did undoubtedly happen, as the examination of Wharram Percy church has shown). The practice may spring from a reverence for the 'church door' itself, for its ceremonial or spiritual significance; it was the place where marriages and certain legal transactions took place.

The chancel arches at Adel and the reset pieces at Felkirk have already been mentioned; the only other *in situ* examples in the county are at Bardsey and Hartshead. The former is probably of early 12th-century date but is extremely plain, very like the inserted tower arch. At Hartshead the chancel arch (**54**) is clearly the product of the same phase as the south door (**55**): the doorway impost decoration reappears on the hoodmould of the arch, which has two orders of chevron; the capitals show the very beginnings of upright leaf-like motifs. The stepped responds have broad attached shafts at each angle, exactly like those at Tong where a 12th-century arch from the previous church (?chancel arch) was reset as the tower arch in the 1727 rebuilding; here the capitals are closer to the traditional scalloped form but the two orders of the arch continue the roll mouldings of the responds.

There is no need to discern any antiquarian or spiritual motivation in the resetting of the Tong arch; it was simply a useful and not unattractive piece of architecture which in any case would be largely hidden by the new gallery. Rather more puzzling is the small and severely plain tower arch at Walton, the only 12th-century relic in a church which otherwise seems to be the product of a single 14th-century building campaign; was it originally a chancel arch? Whether *in situ* or not, its retention is hard to explain. At Elland the chancel arch is of steeply pointed form, but its three orders of voussoirs are all 12th-century work reset, the inner two with various roll mouldings and the outer with a stylised form of beakheads far from the fierce bird and animal masks at Thorp Arch. The architect John Bilson, writing in the 1920s, dated the Elland chancel arch to *c.* 1175 (although it seems to have been reset at a later date) and linked the mouldings to those in the church of Kirkstall

54

55

*The Norman chancel arch (**54**) and south doorway (**55**) at Hartshead evidently belong to the same phase of construction.*

Abbey.[4] A major monastic church clearly served as a source for the introduction of new architectural forms amongst the parish churches round about.

The survival of substantial Norman architectural features is confined to about a dozen of the 69 churches covered in this survey. An uncertain number of others have some remains of Norman fabric. In some cases this is distinguishable by its thickness (0.90 to 1.00m is common) and in others by its masonry type: smallish and quite square blocks coursed in with the angle quoins are one distinctive 12th-century form. In other churches Norman fabric is doubtless concealed by plaster and later facings. The thick pieces of wall at the end of the late medieval nave arcades in Batley church are almost certainly 12th-century work; in the south wall of the nave at Kirkthorpe is a patch of distinctive 12th-century stonework with, on its internal face, part of the round-headed rear arch of an earlier south door. At Featherstone nothing remains visible except for the 12th-century north-west angle quoins of the nave. Masonry in the nave walls of several churches (among them Badsworth, possibly Emley, Swillington and Woolley) is almost certainly of the period, as is the chancel at Otley (which preserves two windows) and probably the north wall of the chancel at South Kirkby. At Calverley the much-scraped nave walls are older than the present arcades; there are remains of a very plain round-headed window in the south wall which could be either Saxon or Norman. A single blocked window, probably later 12th century, is all that visibly survives of the medieval church at Knottingley.

The Norman font at White Chapel, Cleckheaton, includes a sheila-na-gig (Celtic fertility figure) among its decorative motifs. It is the most spectacular remnant of the medieval chapel.

56

Virtually all the parish churches in the county were established by the early 12th century. Where work of this period does not survive, or cannot be recognised, in the standing fabric, there may be *ex situ* evidence: at Badsworth some architectural fragments; at Collingham a reset moulded arch in a churchyard outbuilding; at Halifax a scatter of chevron-moulded voussoirs and other fragments reused throughout the building; some carved stones at Rothwell; architectural fragments lying in the churchyard at Thornhill; the spectacular font of *c.* 1100 at White Chapel (Cleckheaton) (**56**); a carved panel at Wragby; and early medieval cross slabs at Almondbury, Bradford, Dewsbury, Keighley, Sandal Magna and other places.

---

4   J. Bilson, 'Elland church, chancel arch', *Yorkshire Archaeological Journal* 26 (1922), 305-307

CHAPTER FIVE

The Dawning of the Gothic

The question of where the English Gothic style began has been the cause of much debate; its characteristic pointed arch first appears in the high vaults of some of the great 12th-century abbey churches and cathedrals. In due course this radical new development filtered down to the parish churches, where it began to appear in the second half of the 12th century. It is really this change from round to pointed arches that marks out the 'Transitional' style, which went on to develop into the fully grown 'Early English', or what the Victorians called the 'First Pointed', by *c.* 1200; it continued in vogue until the later part of the 13th century. Mouldings became complex, as can be seen in the fine south doorway at Darrington; new forms of ornament such as nail-head and dog-tooth came into common use.

The changes that took place in country churches were not limited to architectural style. During the late 12th and 13th centuries many, if not most, churches had their chancels extended to the east or completely rebuilt. Pre-Conquest and many early Norman churches tended to have small box-like chancels, but developments in ritual meant that these were no longer sufficient for liturgical needs. All these changes took place in West Yorkshire, although often, as with earlier phases of development, they have now been masked by further remodellings which took place later in the medieval period. Aisles continued to be added to earlier naves; they were still little more than narrow walkways, with low external walls. Nave and aisles together would be contained under one steep-pitched 'catslide' roof, covered by wooden shingles or in some cases thatched.

Bardsey, a church we have already followed through its Anglo-Saxon and Norman phases, is a good place to see the beginnings of the Gothic. The south arcade here cannot date from long after 1150 (**57**); although its arches are pointed they are of one plain square order like those on the opposite side, with an almost identical hoodmould. The eastern respond (partly renewed) has two curved volute-like leaves supporting the heavy square abacus, but the returns of the abacus are decorated with sunk 'harp'-shaped ornament (triangles with their lower angles rounded), which has parallels in some pre-Conquest decoration. The piers are still heavy and round.

Transitional work of around 1170 is well seen in Ferrybridge church, which falls into the unusual category of being a medieval church reconstituted on a new site; it originally stood at Ferry Fryston, and was moved in 1952-53. The tower arch is almost but not quite semicircular, and is of one square order; its construction harks back to the Anglo-Saxon tradition of 'through stones'. The west window is a small lancet with a pointed head but a semicircular rear arch. The north door has a double-chamfered arch of strange segmental-pointed form, the outer order resting on jamb shafts

57

which have capitals carved with leaves which have their tips curling over, producing the form known as 'waterleaf'. The hoodmould has nail-head ornament, one of the text-book Early English forms.

There is only one church in West Yorkshire which can be classed as a more or less complete Early English building, and that is Kirkburton. In its present form it is basically a building of *c.* 1200, although as we have seen it embodies the 'ghost' of an earlier structure; sadly it suffered rather heavily from 19th-century improvements and restoration. The fully aisled nave is of six bays; in its original form it had a roof of quite spectacularly steep pitch, the weathering of which remains on the tower. There is an elongate chancel, and a west tower which is clearly an addition. At the angles of south aisle and chancel are quite striking buttresses; those to the aisle are massive, squat, and of square plan, 'clasping' the corners, whilst those at the east end of the chancel are stepped, and set in pairs at right angles to each other. The west door (**61**), reset in the west wall of the tower, has a richly moulded arch: a line of large dog-tooth ornament on the inner order continues down to ground level; nail-head ornament in the outer order is carried on jamb shafts which are themselves flanked by vertical lines of running leaf ornament. The south aisle (the north was rebuilt in 1825) originally had a very low eaves line; nave and aisles must at first have been covered by one great roof. At each end of the aisle, at the original eaves level, is a strange projecting bracket carried on two moulded corbels, and there are similar brackets high on the west gable; it is difficult to reconstruct their function. The chancel windows are all lancets (**58**), with towards the west end of the south wall a pair divided by a shaft with a moulded capital. Most of the stonework here is of 1850, although it is apparently a faithful copy of what was there before: the decayed remains of the original lancet pair now stand in the churchyard (**59**). Inside the church the arcades have octagonal piers except for one puzzling exception, the westernmost pier on the north side, which is round; the capitals are carved with foliage of different forms (**60**), whilst the double-chamfered pointed arches have hoodmoulds with carved stops.

38

58

59

The Early English lancet windows at Kirkburton have been restored (58), but the remains of an original pair of lancets are preserved outside (59). The arcades, with various forms of foliage carved on the capitals (60), and a fine doorway with dog-tooth ornament (61; later reset in the west tower), indicate a date of about 1200.

60

61

62   63

*Two unusual features of the Kirkburton chancel are the screen wall behind the altar (**62**), and the medieval doorway and 'squint' on the north side (**63**).*

The Kirkburton chancel has two intriguing features. The first, on the north, is a shouldered-arched doorway (now giving access to the vestry) with a small window or 'squint' beside it (**63**); on the opposite side of this wall the squint can be seen to be set in a recess provided with a wall-seat. Clearly there was a structure here before the early 20th-century vestry, one which it is tempting to link to the anchoress Agnes, daughter of William de Burton, mentioned in a document of 1293.

The other feature is a screen wall behind the altar (**62**). In its present form this was built in 1907 but it incorporates at each end a 13th-century doorway with filleted roll mouldings and nail-head ornament in the capitals. These are said to have been 'found in the vicarage garden'. It seems possible that the wall and doorways reproduce an original feature. Hodgson Fowler, the Durham architect responsible for the 1907 works was a keen antiquarian, and may have had good reasons for his reconstruction. There are records of a chamber in this position at Dewsbury, and the foundations of a third were revealed during an excavation in Hickleton church, South Yorkshire. These eastern chambers show that the altar was set some distance short of the east end. The position of the altar in a parish church has varied through the ages; in some earlier Anglo-Saxon churches it was set at the east end of the nave, and then in the later Anglo-Saxon period at the west end of the chancel. This slow eastwards migration continued through the medieval period until a position actually against the east wall was reached. Recent excavations at St Peter's church, Barton-on-Humber, have shown that the 10th-century chancel had a timber screen at mid-length, with the altar set against its west face and a chamber beyond. Whatever their function (presumably as a sacristy, but possibly also to house relics, as some interesting finds at Hickleton suggest) these chambers may once have been relatively common. Where screen walls were of timber, however, evidence for their position may come only through archaeological investigation.

The only parts of the medieval church at Dewsbury to have escaped 18th and 19th-century rebuilding are the nave arcades, together with the fragmentary remains of earlier walls above; both are of considerable interest. The south arcade consists of four pointed, double-chamfered arches resting on piers of a quatrefoil or four-lobed section, a development of the same type as seen in the Norman south arcade at Guiseley; their plan differs in having a shallow swept curve in between each adjacent pair of lobes, rather than a right-angled return. The date of the arcade is a matter of

*The 13th-century north arcade at Dewsbury (**64**) has piers formed by five detached shafts; they are remarkably similar in style to the responds for the chancel chapels at Guiseley (**65**).*

64   65

debate among architectural historians; some place it *c.* 1170 whilst others would put it a full century later.[1] This serves to illustrate the problem, more common in the later medieval period, of attributing a stylistic date to features with 'standard' elements (e.g. double-chamfered arches, quatrefoil piers) which remained in use over a long period of time, and lack features or decorative motifs of a more easily datable type. Perhaps the least useful architectural feature as regards dating is the octagonal pier; these were used from soon after 1200 until the end of the medieval period.

The Dewsbury north arcade is quite different. Here the piers are still of a quatrefoil form, but the quatrefoil is formed by five detached shafts, the central a little broader than the four flanking it (**64**). The pier bases have deep 'waterholding' mouldings,[2] and at mid-height the shafts are linked by triple moulded rings. The capitals, too, are richly moulded, but above these the arches are of two chamfered orders, just like the south arcade. The piers and their mouldings are fully developed 'Early English' in style, and they are usually dated to the second quarter of the 13th century.

Guiseley church had chapels, almost like little transepts, added onto either side of its chancel in the 13th century. Their arches (of the usual double-chamfered section) spring from responds which are so similar to the Dewsbury north arcade that it is tempting to see them as the work of the same mason (**65**): each respond has a detached shaft surrounded by three smaller ones, and the

---

1   K. Senior, *Dewsbury Parish Church, All Saints. A short history and guide* (n.d.), places it around 1170, whilst N. Pevsner, *Buildings of England: Yorkshire The West Riding* (1967, 2nd ed.), 179, assigns it to the later 13th century.

2   A self-explanatory term: a deep hollow which would hold water.

The development of windows in the 13th century can be seen by comparing Almondbury (66), where lights are paired and enclosed within a plain pointed arch, with Guiseley (67), where the spaces between and above two pairs of conjoined lights are pierced by trefoil and cusped-circle tracery.

66   67

capital mouldings are identical to those at Dewsbury; the bases however have a much simpler section of three rounded steps.

Arcades probably of 13th-century date are to be found in several other churches – Badsworth, Darrington, Felkirk and Normanton among them – and are recognisable by such features as round piers and 'waterholding' mouldings to the bases; nowhere else do the graceful detached shafts of Dewsbury and Guiseley reappear. The problem of dating such arcades by one or two features is heightened by the fact that some sections – whole piers in some cases, bases and/or capitals in others – may be reused from an earlier phase of the building; this is a practice we have already seen with Norman doorways and chancel arches. At both Wakefield Cathedral and Sandal Magna parish church the nave arcades in their present form seem to be of 14th-century date,[3] but reuse older piers; Bradford Cathedral seems to be a similar case, with 13th-century quatrefoil piers, rather like those of the Dewsbury south arcade, reused in the 14th or early 15th century. At Ilkley a good 13th-century south door, with continuous mouldings of rolls and dog-tooth ornament, was reset when the present south aisle was either added or rebuilt in the later medieval period.

Several chancels show evidence of 13th-century rebuilding. The smaller Anglo-Saxon or Norman chancel at Ledsham was replaced at this period, although its successor suffered heavily in the 19th century. The chancel at Bramham is also a rebuild of this date, and here retains several original lancet windows in the side walls. The windows of late 12th and earlier 13th-century

---

3   Those at Sandal may have been reconstructed a second time in the 17th or 18th century.

churches were usually simple lancets, tall and narrow single lights with pointed arches to their heads; occasionally they might be used in pairs, as at Kirkburton, or triplets. A major development in window form took place in the mid-13th century, in that several lights were combined under one arch. The simplest form of this is seen at Almondbury where the earlier chancel (of uncertain date) seems to have been extended eastwards around 1250; in its side walls, now enclosed by 19th-century chapels, are windows consisting of a pair of lancet-like lights enclosed within a larger pointed arch (**66**); the spandrel of the larger arch is simply a blind panel, without any decoration or piercing. This form of opening had of course previously been used in belfries, for example in the Norman towers at Aberford, Bramham and Ledsham, but rarely as windows in the body of a church.

As far as towers themselves are concerned, it is uncertain how many West Yorkshire churches had them before the great wave of tower building in the later 15th century; few earlier examples survive. Woodkirk is undoubtedly the best 13th-century tower in the county (**68**), and is the only

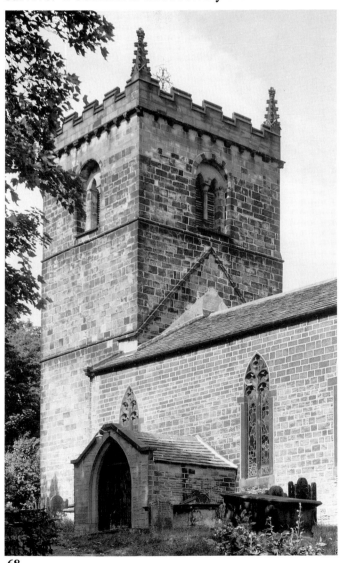

69

68
70

*Woodkirk has the finest 13th-century tower in West Yorkshire (**68**). The tower arch has been altered (**69**), but one fragment of the original foliage decoration on its capitals survives (**70**).*

substantial relic of the small Augustinian priory there; it must date from early in the century, as some of its features are still close to the transition between Romanesque and Gothic. The tower is in three stages divided by string-courses; at its base is a fine plinth of very steep section, capped by a bold roll moulding. On the west side of the lower stage is a single lancet window with a hoodmould showing indented or 'nutmeg' decoration, an ornament close to some Norman forms. The belfry has two-light openings: the individual lights have pointed heads, but they are enclosed under a round arch. The lights are divided by a central octagonal shaft with a simple capital, and also have an impost band which is hollow-chamfered beneath (very much a 12th-century feature), stepping out round the jambs of the outer arch. The double-chamfered tower arch (69) has been mutilated by later alterations, but has originally had capitals with high-quality foliage decoration; all that survives of this, on the tower side of the north respond, is a solitary quite beautifully carved leaf (70).

A handful of church towers in the Pennine west of the county are probably of 13th-century origin, although they, in common with later medieval churches in that region, have an almost 'vernacular' feel, and lack details and ornaments which could be tied in closely with mainstream architectural developments in the lowlands. At Mirfield, the old parish church, the body of which had been converted into a 'preaching box' in 1826, was demolished in the late 19th century except for its medieval west gable and tower (73). Here in the 15th century the old tower had simply been topped with a new belfry stage; the old belfry below it has openings in the forms of quite squat paired lancets. The tower arch is no more than a large pointed doorway with a simple chamfer,

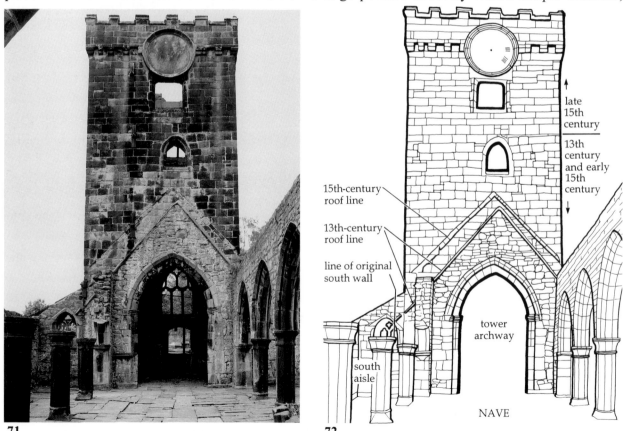

71

72

The lower half of Heptonstall tower has been dated to the 13th century, as has the lower of the two nave roof lines shown on the photograph (71) and key drawing (72).

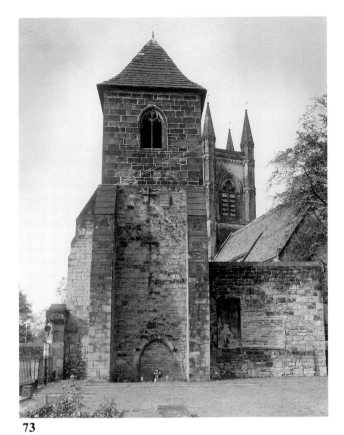

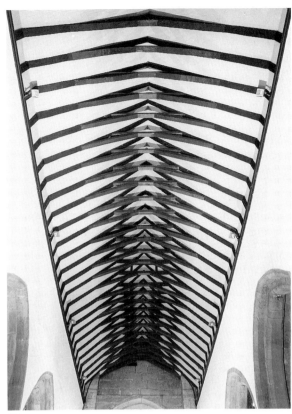

73
           74

The ruined medieval church at Mirfield has a 13th-century tower heightened in the 15th century (73). Its nave roof may originally have been similar to that at Elland (74) which is probably the oldest surviving church roof in West Yorkshire.

continuous round head and jambs. There are no buttresses, string-courses or architectural elaborations whatsoever. At Heptonstall another earlier tower has been heightened by a belfry stage in the 15th century (**71, 72**). This has a little more detail: there is a plinth with roll moulding and stepped buttresses set back from the western angles. The weathering of a very steeply pitched roof with a low eaves line, visible on the east face of the tower, looks typically 13th century as well, but there has been much alteration. The tower at Calverley resembles that at Heptonstall in having a rectangular stair turret projecting from the east end of the south wall, and has a steeply sloped plinth, but has again been subject to a later medieval remodelling.

      Returning to window development, the next stage, and rather an exciting one, is seen in the four-light window in the gable end of the south chapel at Guiseley (**67**), which has been dated to 1260-75. Here a pair of two-light windows, like those at Almondbury except that they have pierced circles with trefoil cusping in their spandrels, are put together side-by-side under a single large arch, which has a larger cusped circle at its apex. Here we have the beginnings of window tracery, the developing and changing styles of which allow us to classify the later phases of Gothic architecture. Not only the multiplicity of lights, but also the use of cusping, to elaborate their form, were to continue to the end of the medieval period. Practically, the development of multiple windows and tracery meant that the interiors of churches became much lighter places; the end result of the trend was, in some parts of the country, to produce great churches in the Perpendicular style which could truly be said to have more window than wall.

The oldest surviving timberwork in any church in West Yorkshire is probably the nave roof at Elland (**74**). This is of a very simple collared-rafter form, not unlike the 13th-century roof structure of part of Elland Hall (now demolished). Each pair of rafters is linked by a collar, and the framework thus produced is strengthened by a long straight strut or brace between the collar and the lower part of the rafter. This is a typical roof structure in the earlier medieval or 'lowland' tradition, where each pair of rafters in effect forms a truss, and there are no strengthening members running lengthwise; later medieval church roofs in the county are in what has been termed the 'highland' tradition, in which the individual rafters are supported by longitudinal timbers – purlins and a ridge – which in turn are supported by trusses composed of much heavier members, set at intervals and dividing the roof into bays. It would be fascinating to know the form taken by the 13th-century roofs of churches like Kirkburton, Heptonstall and Mirfield, where our only evidence is the roof tabling or weathering surviving on the east side of the towers.

75

76

Late 13th-century changes in window design can be seen at Kippax, by comparing the plain two-light window on the south side of the chancel (75) with the intersecting bar tracery of the east window (76).

CHAPTER SIX

The Late 13th and 14th Centuries

In church architecture the later 13th and most of the 14th century are characterised by the Decorated or 'Middle Pointed' style, the second of the main phases of the English Gothic; differences in the developing styles of window tracery allow architectural historians to make further sub-divisions or classifications such as 'geometrical', 'reticulated' (net-like) and 'flowing'. More complex arch mouldings appear, in particular, rolls embellished with square-section fillets, and in carved detail representations of foliage are more closely copied from nature. Whilst these changes in tracery style, mouldings and ornament are all well seen in the country's 'great churches', coming down to the more humble level of the parish church they are often less apparent; the so-called standard elements, such as arcades with octagonal piers and double-chamfered arches, continued in use throughout the period and beyond. Evidence of Decorated work is usually best seen in windows, but these have often been altered, or been subjected to a well-meaning 19th-century restoration which need not necessarily follow their original form. Square-headed windows come into vogue for the first time and can be seen in many churches, for example at Bardsey. Two new forms of arch come into common use: one is the ogee, formed from two wave-like curves, a type that remained in use into the 15th century, and reappears again 200 years after that in the vernacular architecture of the region; the other is the shouldered form, which occurs occasionally even before the Norman Conquest, but only became popular in the 14th century.

Kippax church was remodelled, apparently after a serious fire, in the later 13th century when the Early English style was giving way to the Decorated. On the south side of the chancel is a two-light window with an unpierced spandrel (**75**), very like the chancel windows at Almondbury, but the east window is of four lights with intersecting bar tracery (**76**); this seems to be genuine medieval work, although the window design is one which, like the simple Y-tracery of some two-light windows of the same period, re-emerged in the late 18th and early 19th centuries and has led some quite eminent architectural historians astray. The window has a triple-chamfered surround both internally and externally, the glass being set close to the centre of the wall. This symmetry as regards internal and external faces is seen again in the early to mid-14th-century east windows to the chancel (**77**) and south chapel (**78**) at Hemsworth; these are of five and three lights, and are excellent examples of flowing and reticulated tracery, respectively. They are in fact the only pre-19th-century features on the whole of the external elevations of the church. Inside the chancel at Kippax is an apparently unique triple piscina cut into the south-east corner; it has two moulded arches, one in each wall, carried on a short shaft with a moulded capital and base set in the wall angle.

77 78

Hemsworth church contains two fine 14th-century windows with flowing tracery (77) and reticulated tracery (78).

Several of the larger parish churches in the county had developed to almost their present size before 1350, although all underwent substantial changes in the next two centuries. A major rebuilding of Wakefield church (now the cathedral) is thought to have been prompted by a collapse of the old central tower; the recorded consecration of a chapel in 1329 has been correlated with the reopening of the church after these works. Subsequent rebuilding of the eastern arm, and much post-medieval alteration have left little of the 14th-century work intact except for the nave arcades and chancel arch, which have quadrant and wave mouldings. The new piers of the north arcade (which also incorporates two 12th-century piers) show another variant on the common quatrefoil theme, with each lobe forming in effect a wave moulding with a broad square-ended keel.

Nearby St Helen's parish church at Sandal Magna was being remodelled at about the same time, once again reusing old piers in the nave arcades; the new arches were simple ones of two chamfered orders, although some of the new pier capitals have quite complex mouldings. The crossing arches were remodelled, the old responds being heightened and new arches constructed; each of these has two sunk wave mouldings. A few 14th-century windows survive. Two now in the east end of the chancel (which, like Almondbury, is rather an oddity in having three separate windows) have two trefoil-headed lights with a cusped panel in the spandrel of the same shape as one finds in larger windows with reticulated tracery (**79**). The windows in the aisle walls are of two and three lights, both lights and enclosing arches having flat shouldered heads, a rather inelegant form that occasionally occurs at this time. The original belfry openings (below the added

48

15th-century belfry) have twin arched lights without cusping, with the spandrel above left open under an enclosing arch; the surrounds of both individual lights and enclosing arch have a surprisingly complex moulding of rolls and hollows. All in all the windows are an odd variety, and suggest that the 14th-century alterations took place in more than one phase.

An unusual feature at Sandal is the means of access to the central tower: a staircase at the north-west corner of the north transept leads up to a little slab-roofed gallery running along the top of the transept west wall, to give access to a conventional newel stair in the north-west corner of the tower; the gallery is lit by two little shouldered-arched windows looking down into the transept.

A similar high-level gallery is seen at Darrington, a church which preserves some of the best Decorated work in the county (**80**). The gallery here is reached by a newel stair in a turret at the north-west corner of the early 14th-century chapel on the north side of the chancel; the stair goes on past the gallery to end with a doorway onto the chapel roof, and a moulded capital-like block, resting on the top of the newel, which supports a roof of flat wedge-shaped slabs laid radially. The limestone blocks of the turret interior show good specimens of bolster tooling, which seems to correlate with 13th and 14th-century fabric. Descending again to the gallery, this has an arcade of three segmental-pointed arches on each side, looking down into both the north nave aisle and the north chancel chapel (and incidentally providing a good view of the unusual roof structure of the latter, in which the place of roof trusses is taken by eight chamfered stone arches carrying the

79   80

*Sandal Magna chancel has a pair of 14th-century windows in its east wall (*79*). The church also has a high-level gallery, like the one at Darrington (*80*).*

longitudinal timbers). The gallery now ends against a curving face of blank wall, plastered over. Its purpose remains a mystery: does the curve of the end wall, which is clearly an original feature as the arches in the side walls have been made of disproportionate width to allow for it, relate to a blocked newel stair? The whole arrangement might be connected with a central tower that was never built, or, perhaps more likely, with rood loft arrangements. Turning away from such mysteries, Darrington church has some fine three-light windows with reticulated tracery, and a frieze of cusped panels, just above the plinth on the south side of the chancel, which also seems to be of 14th-century date.

Reticulated patterns developed into flowing tracery, perhaps the most elegant of the Decorated forms. The east window at Calverley, with its sinuous flame-like forms, is probably the best example in the county, although in its present state it is an 1870 copy of the original (**81**). If the mid-14th-century chancel here had not been rebuilt (with some 'improvements': the chancel arch was widened and the number of recesses in the sedilia increased from two to three) it would have been classed as one of the best pieces of architecture of the period in the area. The tower west window is a simpler three-light essay in the same style, and does appear to be original (**82**).

All Saints at Pontefract is another big cruciform church which, like Wakefield and Sandal, had already reached its present size by the first half of the 14th century (**83**). Sadly an over-active

81   **82**

*Flowing tracery can be seen at Calverley, in the east window (**81**) and the tower window (**82**)*

83

involvement in the Civil War sieges of the nearby castle has left the church largely a roofless ruin; although much of the shell still stands, its architectural features are in poor condition. There are hints of earlier work in the nave, and 13th-century fabric in the chancel, but otherwise the bulk of the building is of the earlier 14th century. The windows of the aisles and nave clerestory have decaying remains of richly moulded surrounds, and a few fragments of reticulated tracery hang from the arches of those on the south side of the Lady Chapel. As already noted, 14th-century builders in West Yorkshire produced some original variants on the theme of stairs and access to towers, but none more unusual than at Pontefract. The church has a lofty crossing tower, repaired and restored by the Leeds architect Robert Chantrell in 1831, which has a stair turret at its north-west corner. This contains what has been termed a 'double-helix' newel stair; in effect two separate stairs wind around the same central newel, one entered from a doorway on the north, in the aisle, and one from the nave to the south. At the present top of the turret (before 1831 it continued higher) the two stairs unite; the present arrangement is a hinged trapdoor which can be swung to allow access from one stair or the other to a short flight of steps cut through the thickness of the wall into the ringing chamber. The tower is itself tall, but is capped by an octagonal lantern which seems to have been added late in the 14th century; unfortunately this collapsed in 1660 as a result of war damage, and was rebuilt, considerably lower, in the late 17th century. In its medieval form the tower must have been extremely impressive, in appearance something like a larger-scale version of the lantern tower at All Saints, Pavement, in York.

The old St Peter's church at Leeds, pulled down in 1838, was another quite large cruciform church mainly of 14th-century date. Halifax probably had a similar large church, possibly cruciform, by this period as well, but here the 15th-century remodelling has obliterated all but a few tantalising traces of the older building. The only 14th-century architectural features to survive are three windows in the north wall of the north aisle. These are each of two lights with quite steeply pointed trefoiled heads; there is an uncusped open panel in the spandrel. As at Kippax and Hemsworth, the glass-line is set close to the centre of the wall, but here the inner frame is provided with two roll mouldings whilst the outer is a plain but broad chamfer.

Swillington church, known to any motorist on the A642 by its distinctive 'two tone' appearance, has a 15th-century west tower of smoke-blackened gritstone and a late 14th-century body of white magnesian limestone; the arcades are of standard elements and the windows of two and three lights, with flowing tracery which was mostly renewed last century. Everything is relatively plain and simple; there is a little more elaboration in the sedilia with their cusped ogee arches, although these too look largely 19th century; more genuine is the tomb recess in the south aisle, which has an ogee arch with multiple cusping and mouldings including a line of small square flowers.

A much finer tomb recess is one of the best features of St Peter's church at Walton, which is a small but good-quality building that must class as the most complete Decorated church in West Yorkshire. Formerly a chapel of Thorp Arch, the present church, with the exception of a Norman tower arch and a 16th-century belfry, seems to have been built in the second quarter of the 14th century. It consists only of nave, chancel and west tower, with a later vestry and south porch. The south doorway has a surprisingly large arch with a continuous double-wave moulding (**85**); the nave windows are each of two trefoil-headed lights with pierced spandrels, under square frames and hoodmoulds with head stops . The chancel has fine east (five-light) (**87**) and south (three-light) windows with excellent reticulated tracery, as at Darrington; further west in the south wall are a priest's door and a 'low-side' window (**84**), both with shouldered arches. There was formerly a 'low-side' on the north as well, now reset in the late 19th-century organ chamber.

Low-side windows, which are more common in some parts of the country than in others, have aroused considerable antiquarian controversy. They are usually set at the west end of the south wall of the chancel and have been explained as places for lanterns to frighten away evil spirits, places where sacring bells were rung during the Mass, or openings where lepers could receive the consecrated elements without entering the church. The only other pair of such windows in West Yorkshire is in the early 14th-century chancel at Bardsey where, because of later additions, both now open internally. There is another example, also 14th century but this time of two lights, at Adel, one of the few inserted features permitted to survive the Victorian re-Normanisation there. In some cases the sill of an otherwise conventional window in this position might be extended downwards, as in the case of a lancet at Ledsham (renewed in 1871 but copying an older feature) and a similar window at Bramham which did not survive the 19th-century restoration there.

The tomb recess at Walton, by far the most spectacular feature of the interior, is set on the north side of the chancel and has a cusped arch under a panelled ogee-shaped canopy flanked by tall pinnacles; there is carved foliage in the spandrels of the cusping (**86**). The quite slender west tower is surprisingly plain; perhaps the vicissitudes of the mid-14th century, the terrible Black Death and associated economic troubles, affected the planned building programme.

There is one more building that must be considered here, although in its present form it can hardly be considered a medieval structure. This is the Wakefield Bridge Chantry, known to have

Walton, the most complete 14th-century church in West Yorkshire, includes a shouldered 'low-side' window (84), a south doorway with continuous double-wave moulding (85), a spectacular tomb recess (86), and an east window with reticulated tracery (87).

84

85

86

87

been under construction in the 1340s and in use, despite a possible break in construction occasioned by the Black Death, by 1356 (**88**). It is quite a small building (12.80 by 5.10m internally), attached to the medieval bridge, and in fact built on a small mid-stream island in the River Calder. The west facade is the finest aspect of the building, being divided by buttresses into seven narrow bays; there are three doorways, alternating with recessed panels carved with flowing tracery, all set under crocketed ogee canopies beneath taller triangular panels or pediments, against a background of more tracery and diaper work. The parapet above, between big pinnacles with canopied niches, has a series of carved panels depicting the Annunciation, Nativity, Resurrection, Ascension and Pentecost (replacing the Coronation of the Virgin). The side walls each have three, three-light windows with flowing tracery under square heads, and at the east end is a similar five-light window under a low triangular head. At the north-east corner is a stair turret linking chapel and basement sacristy, and continuing up to the roof where it was originally capped by a crown of flying buttresses; the side walls are capped by an elaborate panelled parapet, a feature which reappears in the following century in the great parish churches at Halifax and at Wakefield itself. Inside there are carved canopies above a recess for a stoup in the west wall, and an image niche and the door to the stair turret on either side of the altar at the east end; there is also an elaborate piscina in the south wall.

The chantry chapel of St Mary-on-the-Bridge, as it appears to have been known, is a spectacular piece of architecture, but sadly everything described above is reconstruction or restoration; original stonework survives only in the walls of the basement. The chapel passed through a variety of uses after the medieval period, and was in a ruinous condition when restored in 1847-48 by Mr (later Sir) George Gilbert Scott; it had already undergone 'repairs' in 1797 when the traceried windows were replaced by sashes. Scott's restoration seems to have amounted to a complete reconstruction. The architect had intended merely to repair the worn and damaged west facade, but the stone carver he employed persuaded him to accept an entirely new front made out of soft Caen stone, whilst a local gentleman bought the original to set up as a 'romantic ruin' fronting a boat house by the lake at Kettlethorpe Hall, 4km to the south. It was not long before Scott bitterly and quite openly regretted the deal: 'I am filled with wonder to think how I ever was induced to consent to it at all' he wrote 30 years later. By that time the Caen stone had rotted so fast in the polluted atmosphere of the industrial West Riding that it was in a worse state than the original magnesian limestone facade had ever been. Scott himself instigated the first of several schemes to return the old stonework to the chapel, but none ever came to fruition.

The disintegrating remains of the Caen stone facade were replaced in 1939 by another new front, this time of gritstone; within recent years much of Scott's window tracery in the side walls has had to be replaced as well. The present facade remains an impressive piece of carving, but neither it nor the chapel behind has any real air of antiquity. Meanwhile, the most ornate piece of 14th-century architecture in West Yorkshire still stands above the reeds and above its reflection in the lake at Kettlethorpe, making, as Sir Nikolaus Pevsner observed, the 'most precious of all boat-houses'.[1]

---

1   N. Pevsner, *Buildings of England: Yorkshire The West Riding* (1967, 2nd ed.), 535

88
The facade of Wakefield Bridge chantry chapel, removed to the grounds of Kettlethorpe Hall in the 19th century.

89

Halifax church, largely rebuilt in the 15th and 16th centuries, contains much fine Perpendicular architecture. The remarkable font cover is also in the Perpendicular style.

CHAPTER SEVEN

Prosperity and Pennine Perpendicular

When historians discuss the 'vernacular' buildings of an area, the houses and cottages built of local materials in regional styles, they often invoke the concept of a 'Great Rebuilding'. What this means is that there was a fixed, relatively short period during which virtually all the buildings in an area were rebuilt. In the Pennine Dales inscriptions above farmhouse doorways show that the 20 to 30 year period over which their Great Rebuilding took place varied from valley to valley. When it comes to medieval church buildings, similar periods of activity can be identified, varying from region to region. The second half of the 14th century, after the depredations of the Scottish wars and plagues, was understandably a time when relatively little church building was carried out. By the mid-15th century, however, the Great Rebuilding of West Yorkshire churches, a phase which was to span 70 or 80 years, had begun.

The amount of money being spent on church buildings at one time or another is often a better indicant of the prosperity of the local inhabitants, than of their piety. With developing industries, notably textile production, and changes in the old tenurial patterns under which land was held, more money was available; this is reflected in the number of surviving wills that record money being left to the fabric of local parish churches. The enlargement and remodelling of West Yorkshire churches in the later 15th and early 16th centuries is matched by the rebuilding and enlargement of many houses in the area, usually of timber-framed construction.[1]

This upsurge of interest in church building expressed itself in the third of the styles of the English Gothic, the Perpendicular or 'Third Pointed'. In window tracery the patterns changed from the reticulated and flowing motifs of the Decorated style to more geometrical tiers and grids of panels. The visual emphasis was now on the vertical mullion rather than the curved line, hence the term 'Perpendicular'. In some larger windows the horizontal transom, often with embattled or crenellated ornament, appears. A common form is to have a range of sub-lights forming the head of the window, two to each of the main lights below; simple forms like this are classed as 'panel tracery' (**89, 90**). In some later Perpendicular windows, when the style is passing into the more loosely defined Tudor (or what some writers used to call 'debased' Perpendicular), cuspings are omitted from the heads of lights, and in the tracery mullions are often continued straight up to join the curve of the arch, without any shaped head to the sub-light at all. Windows like this can be seen at Featherstone and Felkirk (east end of chancel), and at Normanton at the east end of the south

---

1   RCHME, *Rural Houses of West Yorkshire, 1400-1830* (1986, Supplementary Series 8, Royal Commission on the Historical Monuments of England, West Yorkshire Metropolitan County Council)

90

91

*Two dated Perpendicular windows at Thornhill (**90**; dated 1499) and Normanton (**91**; c. 1519).*

92

93

*Crofton's porch roof (**92**) was built in the early 15th century, as were South Kirkby's tower arch responds with carved foliage (**93**).*

chapel (**91**), which is presumably the 'newe quere of our most blyssede Ladye' referred to in the 1519 will of George Friston.[2] The south windows of the Normanton chapel, and many other windows at Felkirk, Batley and other churches, have lights with round or elliptical heads within chamfered square frames. It is sometimes difficult to ascertain whether very simple forms like this are original (and if they are, whether they are of late medieval or post-medieval date) or the result of cusping being cut away, perhaps to facilitate the insertion of new glass, at a later date. The 'casement' moulding, a wide hollow, can sometimes be used as an indicant of genuine late 15th and early 16th-century work.

Externally, other hallmarks of a typical West Yorkshire church of this period are features such as clerestories, embattled parapets, low-pitched roofs (made possible by the increasing use of lead as a roofing material), and west towers with corbelled-out parapets and angle pinnacles. South porches in which a stone slab roof is carried on a series of chamfered arched ribs are another characteristic, and are to be seen at Crofton (**92**), Featherstone, Felkirk, Hemsworth (rebuilt), Heptonstall, Methley, Normanton and Whitkirk. This type has earlier origins, appearing in the 14th century at Darrington.

Inside the church the 'standard' elements of arcades, chancel and tower arches all continue, although four-centred and flat-pointed arches gain in popularity at the expense of the earlier two-centred and more steeply pointed type. Foliage carving tends to become more formalised, the vigorous naturalistic leaf and flower forms of the 14th century being reduced to repetitive ornament such as the 'square flowers' seen on the capitals of the chancel arcade at Elland and the tower arches at Barwick in Elmet, Swillington, and elsewhere. Rather better-quality carved foliage forms are found on the tower arch responds at South Kirkby (**93**), a church which was remodelled, with quite an amount of good carved detail, early in the 15th century. The ogee forms of the crocketed gablets on the tower buttresses, and the canopy over the west door, hark back to the previous century. Even more surprising is the dog-tooth ornament in the outer order of the west door; it is difficult to see whether this is reset older material, a 15th-century revival of a 13th-century form, or simply an incorrect Victorian restoration.

Turning from the architectural detail to the plans of churches, Perpendicular buildings show a tendency towards the fully developed aisled rectangle. In West Yorkshire this is invariably the end result of additions and alterations to an earlier fabric, rather than a newly introduced form. In other parts of the country, for example in the more northerly Pennine Dales of Craven, groups of late medieval churches are found in which fully aisled bodies have no structural division between nave and chancel; all the West Yorkshire churches of the period retain their chancel arches. Churches with full-length aisles (including those where one chancel aisle or chapel has a vestry at its east end) are seen at Batley, Felkirk, Halifax, Hemsworth, Heptonstall, South Kirkby, Thornhill, Wakefield, Whitkirk, Woolley and Wragby. In a second group the church is fully aisled except for the eastern bay of the chancel, as at Almondbury, Bingley, Bradford (before the recent extensions), Elland and Harewood.

Most churches which had received the old type of narrow aisle in the 12th or 13th century had these rebuilt and widened in the later medieval period; the functional emphasis of the aisle had

---

2   G.E. Kirk, *The Parish Church of Normanton, Yorkshire* (1934), 11

94   95

The almost identical west towers of Rothwell (94) and Barwick (95) were both built about 1460.

now shifted from a route for a procession to an extension of the body of the church needed to accommodate an increasing congregation. At Bardsey the west elevation demonstrates the later medieval widening of 12th-century aisles. In the eastern parts of the church, sacristies and vestries are a common late medieval addition to the chancel, as the position of the rather mysterious eastern chambers, such as those at Dewsbury and Kirkburton, had now been taken by the altar. Vestries and sacristies merit further study, although they have proved particularly susceptible to post-medieval demolition and rebuilding.

Virtually every parish church in the area had acquired a west tower by the 15th century; Adel seems to be the only exception. It is not clear whether these late medieval towers replaced bell-cotes, belfries or earlier towers. The building of new towers is clearly linked to the increasing prosperity of the region, but it also relates to advances in campanalogical technology: bells were now being hung and swung in bell frames (Walton has one of the few medieval frames to survive), rather than simply being suspended on a beam and chimed. More than 30 West Yorkshire churches have wholly Perpendicular west towers, and several others have towers that were altered or heightened during this period, among them Batley, Birstall, Calverley, Heptonstall, Kippax, Mirfield and Sandal. One group of churches in the east of the county, Rothwell (**94**), Barwick in Elmet (**95**), Normanton (**96**), Thorner (**97**) and Whitkirk, have virtually identical towers. Each has a moulded plinth and tall stepped diagonal buttresses, with the only set-back being at the base of the belfry. The embattled

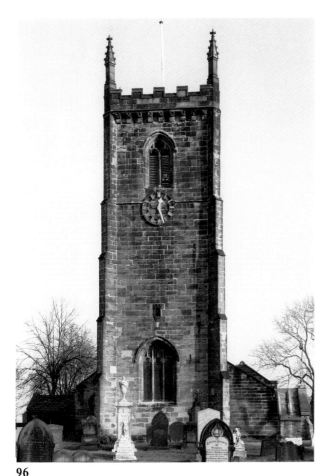 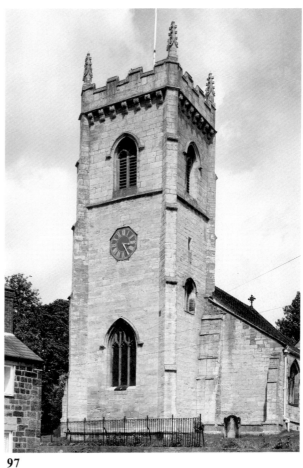

96 97

Normanton (96) and Thorner (97) are further examples of the 'eastern group' of Perpendicular towers.

parapet, which has a crocketed pinnacle at each corner, is set forward on moulded corbels which incorporate drainage spouts; all have three-light west windows and two-light belfry openings. The stairs are set in internal projections cutting off the south-west corner. The main variation lies in whether the tower has a west door or not: only Normanton has no door, although that at Thorner has been blocked and virtually erased externally; the west door at Whitkirk has rather more elaborate mouldings than those at Barwick and Rothwell. Other differences are in minor detail, such as the tracery of the west window and whether the belfry lights are trefoil or cinquefoil-headed. Swillington seems to be another member of the group, although its tower (refaced in 1884) has some rather superior details such as panel decoration on the buttresses.

The Barwick tower is dated to 1455 by an inscribed panel, and at Rothwell we know that there was a bequest of 10 marks towards the fabric of the tower in 1460. The whole group are probably of about the same period; it is interesting to speculate whether they are the work of one team of builders, or whether some form of copy book circulated. A comparison of the detailed dimensions of the towers might be instructive. Further to the west, Guiseley (**99**) also has a mid-15th-century tower which is very similar to the Barwick group. The tower at Batley has a corbelled-out parapet but no angle buttresses. Several writers have likened these overhanging parapets to machicolations in castles, and suggested a possible defensive function; there are no grounds for this assumption. At Batley the stone slabs between the corbels have been removed, giving the impression of

98   99

*Perpendicular towers at Emley (**98**) and Guiseley (**99**), the latter an outlier of the 'eastern group' of towers.*

machicolation, but the corbels themselves (both here and in the eastern group of towers) incorporate drainage spouts, which of course would be unnecessary if the 'machicolation' had been original.

One striking feature of West Yorkshire churches, and one that has never been studied in any detail, is the number of surviving late medieval roofs and ceilings. The majority of these fall into the period which we are now looking at, and the 'highland' tradition of carpentry; the only exception, the 13th-century nave roof at Elland, has already been mentioned.

The most common roof type is that using king-post trusses, the king-post carrying a ridge-piece and the principal rafters supporting two or three levels of purlins. All the timbers are of heavy scantling. Where the roof structure is exposed, it is almost always functional rather than decorative; the open cusped panels at Methley, set between tie-beam and principals, and in the spandrels of braces from the wall-posts, are an exception. At Bingley the roof trusses seem to have been infilled: in the triangle between tie, king-post and principal, a pair of struts cross in an 'X' form, all neatly morticed and pegged together. A recurring theme is the appearance of an intermediate 'truss' midway along each bay. Sometimes this is a true truss, but of simple principal rafter form without a king-post, as at Rothwell and, before 19th-century restorers decided they really ought to have king-posts as well, at Kirkburton. In other cases the intermediate 'truss' has no tie-beam, but consists of a pair of heavier rafters linked by a horizontal member just below the ridge, as at Addingham (**100**), Methley and Ilkley. The chancel at Halifax has, above the panelled ceiling, a roof structure in which conventional king-post trusses alternate with principal rafter types, in which the principals or blades are shaped to an arch-like form.

As roof structures usually lack any ornament or 'architectural' detail it is hard to date them stylistically; recent research into the roofs of late medieval houses in the region may help here. There is of course the potential for accurately dating these roofs using dendrochronology, should resources become available. Occasionally it may be possible to correlate specific forms of roof structure, or elements within those structures, from one church of known date to another where the date of the roof is unknown. At Normanton the south chancel chapel described as 'newe' in 1519 has a king-post roof with the unusual feature of curved or arched wind-braces between the principal rafters and purlins. Arched wind-braces occur again in the rather puzzling nave roof at Emley, which has collar-beam trusses: is this early 16th-century work as well? At Emley a smaller-scale version of the nave roof, also with wind-braces, is seen over the south porch; at Rothwell the porch roof

100
King-post roof trusses at Addingham typify late medieval church roofs in West Yorkshire.

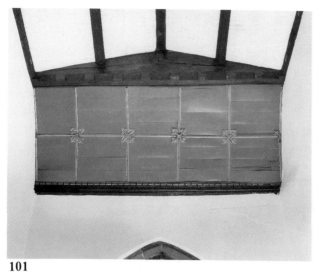

101

102

*South Kirkby retains a coved canopy above the site of the rood loft (**101**); Badsworth has an arch-braced roof (**102**) datable to about 1400.*

structure has collar-beam trusses. The present roofs at Woolley are all 19th century with the exception of that over the porch, which is a surprisingly sophisticated little piece with king-post trusses, moulded tie-beams and moulded rafters. The use of the king-post roof continued long after the end of the medieval period. The low and heavy roof structure at Hartshead has some medieval motifs, such as the cusped arched braces between king-posts and ridge; but it is probably of 17th-century date. At Wragby the nave roof is of king-post type, and is given an air of antiquity by its roughly cut timbers; yet it may be no older than 1811, when it is recorded that new plaster ceilings were constructed.

A rarity survives at South Kirkby in the form of the coved canopy above the rood loft (**101**). This has moulded and embattled top and bottom rails, and is divided into square panels with gilded foliage at the intersections of the timbers. In form it is very close to the dais canopy one would find above the high table in the hall of a gentry house of the period; the canopy at New Hall, Elland (a house built *c.* 1490) had an embattled lower rail.[3] In its original form the panels of the South Kirkby canopy doubtless carried paintings; its secular equivalent would probably have been used for a display of heraldry.

The chancel at Badsworth has a very fine open roof which, like the window tracery and other features of the church, shows that the major remodelling here took place around 1400 (**102**), when elements of both Decorated and Perpendicular styles were current. There are no tie-beams, but long moulded arch braces rising from wall corbels to collars, which carry upper or 'short' king-posts. An unusual feature is the use of 'butt' purlins, longitudinal timbers which are morticed into the faces of the principals rather than carried over their backs. In contrast to all this, the nave roof in the same church is of a simple and plain king-post type, concealed by a contemporary ceiling with a grid of moulded timbers dividing each of its five bays into eight smaller panels.

---

3   RCHME, *Rural Houses of West Yorkshire, 1400-1830* (1986, Supplementary Series 8, Royal Commission on the Historical Monuments of England, West Yorkshire Metropolitan County Council), 196

103

Rothwell nave has a fine decorated late medieval ceiling, but with an inappropriate modern colour scheme.

These late medieval panelled ceilings are surprisingly common in West Yorkshire (about fifteen survive); originally most have been decorated with polychrome bosses at the intersections of the timbers, and possibly by paintings within the panels as well. The Perpendicular trend for ranges of clerestory windows, and indeed for larger windows all round, encouraged the decoration of ceilings which would have been all but invisible in the gloom of the earlier medieval church. It is often difficult to tell whether the carved bosses, or the painted and gilded corbels which carry the wall-posts of a roof (like the dramatic angels over the nave at Bradford), are genuine medieval work or 19th-century restoration; quite a number of roofs, including that over the nave at Badsworth, show the scars of removed bosses. Sometimes a decorated ceiling will survive, as at Rothwell (**103**) (nave) and Featherstone (chancel), when the remainder of the church has been heavily altered or even partly rebuilt; during the 17th and 18th centuries such a ceiling might be underdrawn and concealed by plaster, to be rediscovered and restored at a later date.

Wakefield Cathedral has good late 15th-century ceilings to both its nave and chancel; the nave ceiling seems contemporary with the mid-15th-century clerestory and with a moulded stone cornice,

65

104

105

*The decorated ceiling at Almondbury (**104**) is dated by a surrounding inscription to 1522. The symbols on its bosses include a Green Man (**105**; centre).*

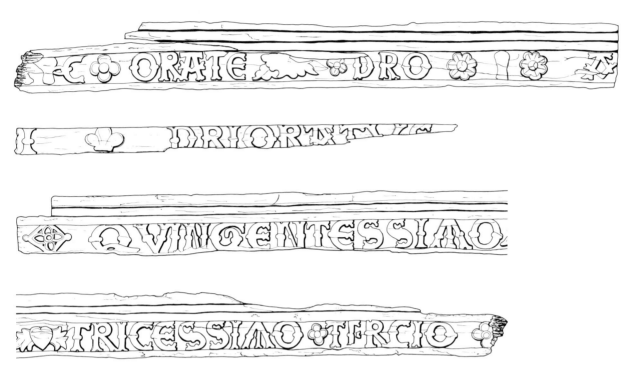

0 — 500 mm

106

Drawings of fragments of the inscribed boards formerly in Wragby church. The inscription refers to Prior Alured of Nostell, and bears the date 1533.

itself with carved bosses, at wall-head level. The chancel ceiling is of similar date; both ceilings have moulded beams with variously carved bosses.

Perhaps the most dramatic of the late medieval ceilings in the area is that at All Hallows, Almondbury (**104, 105**). The Perpendicular remodelling of the church here seems to have spanned at least 30 years: there was an Indulgence for the repair of the building granted in 1486, but the nave ceiling is dated to 1522. The bosses show a variety of the Emblems of the Passion, initials which probably relate to local benefactors, and the common 'Green Man' towards the west end. A long inscription, now regilded, runs round the roof-plates and end tie-beams. The main text is a poem, in English, describing the Passion, and ending with an injunction against swearing. The verses are interrupted by the maker's name: 'Geferay Daystn was the maker of this', and the date.

Wragby church (**106**) also has an inscription on the wall-plates and tie-beams of a ceiling, this time in the chancel. It is a 19th-century copy of the original boards which were taken down and stored, until recently, in a nearby outbuilding. The inscription requests, in Latin, prayers for the soul of Prior Alured (Comyn) of the neighbouring Nostell Priory, and gives the date 1533. As at Almondbury the bosses figure the Emblems of the Passion and, again towards the west end, the 'Green Man'. There has been much speculation on the purpose of this and similar grotesque masks; whatever their function, and whether carved on a roof or on a hoodmould corbel, there seems to have been a tendency to site them towards the west end of nave, aisle or chancel, as far as possible from the altar.

67

107

108

109

Harewood church (107) was built in the first quarter of the 15th century. It contains an outstanding collection of late medieval alabaster monuments (108, 109).

The 15th and 16th centuries, unlike those which went before, provide quite a number of firm dates for additions and alterations to churches, both from documents and from inscriptions on stone, timber and glass. We have already seen two towers and two roofs for which dates are known. A selection of the more important churches of the period are described below; the list is not exhaustive as Perpendicular work, in one form or another, occurs in virtually every old church in the county.

Harewood church stands alone in the park of Harewood House, near the site of the medieval village; it is now in the care of the Redundant Churches Fund. The church has a nave with aisles extending west to flank the west tower, and a chancel with flanking chapels (**107**). The building may incorporate earlier remains (there are a number of odd joints in the masonry, changes in level of the plinth and other minor puzzling features), but as it stands it is wholly Perpendicular, dating to the first quarter of the 15th century, except for a few minor late 18th-century 'improvements' in the form of the present embattled parapets and the quatrefoil window in the east gable. The windows have fairly simple panel tracery and the nave arcades have arches of two chamfered orders which die straight into the octagonal piers; it is not entirely clear whether this absence of capitals is an original feature or the product of some undocumented alteration in the 18th or early 19th century.

Harewood church is most famous for its collection of late medieval alabaster monuments, unrivalled in the north of England (**108, 109**). The chapels flanking the chancel were obviously built to house chantries founded by local families; each has a tomb recess in the form of a segmental-pointed arch cut through the wall between chapel and chancel to the east of the main arch communicating between the two parts. The arches are double-chamfered, without any elaboration; they now house the monuments of Sir Richard Redman (on the north) and Sir William Ryther (on

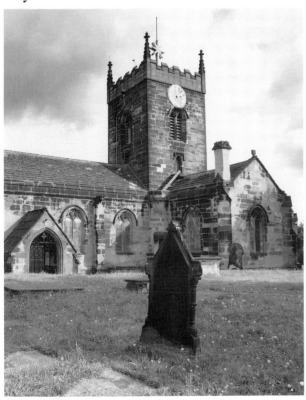

110

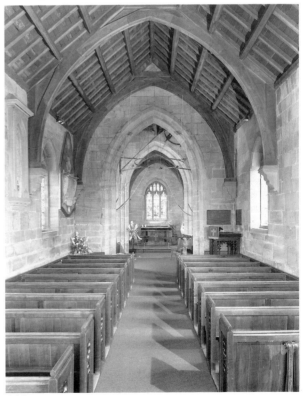

111

*The cruciform-plan church at Crofton (**110**, **111**) remains much as it was built in the early 15th century.*

69

112

Corbels supporting the 15th-century parapets at Whitkirk are carved as grotesque masks.

the south), both more or less contemporary with the building. Each chapel had its own piscina, and a pair of image niches with crocketed canopies on either side of its east window.

Crofton is another early 15th-century church. It is a small cruciform structure, with a central tower (**110**). Like Harewood it is a good-quality but relatively plain building (**111**). The unusual plan and the fact that this is a church all of one date lend support to the strong local tradition that it was built *c.* 1430 by Richard Fleming, Bishop of Lincoln, as a gift to his native village. In the same way, the church at Skirlaugh, 10km north-west of Hull, was built by Bishop Skirlaw of Durham in 1401.

Whitkirk, like Harewood, is a Perpendicular church incorporating no more than the ghost of an older building. Here the founding of a chantry *c.* 1448 and a bequest for new bells in 1454 suggest that the remodelling had taken place around the middle of the century. The window tracery is very like Harewood; one of the features of the church is that the parapets of the tower, nave clerestory and aisles are all set on moulded corbels, some carved as grotesque masks (**112**). The arcades are very much of the standard West Yorkshire type, except that the blocks of masonry at the eastern angles of the nave, carrying arches springing in all four directions, are in the form of large octagonal piers (as at Wragby) with the broader diagonal faces each bearing a pair of broad hollow or casement mouldings.

Repairs in the 1950s revealed the stair which formerly gave access to the rood loft at Whitkirk. This is set in the north wall; a square-headed doorway at the north-west corner of the chancel chapel opens onto a stair, which curves up behind the respond of the arch dividing chapel from aisle, to an upper doorway at the east end of the aisle. Several other churches have 15th-century rood stairs in this position: at Almondbury it is blocked up but fragmentary remains of its two doorways are visible; at Badsworth it is also blocked; and at Bradford and South Kirkby it is hidden by plaster internally but visible as a broad buttress-like projection externally. At Crofton the stair is set in a rounded turret between the aisleless nave and south transept; an 1836 plan shows a similar turret in the angle of chancel and south transept at Otley, which might either have served the rood loft or have been constructed as a post-medieval gallery access. At Batley the stair remains intact in the thickness of the east respond of the south arcade.

Old photographs of Ferry Fryston church show the remains of an opening, presumably the upper door of a rood stair, above an odd doorway-like feature cutting through the east respond of

113
The Waterton Chapel in Methley church is the most impressive chantry chapel to survive in West Yorkshire.

the north arcade – this was presumably a modification of the lower door. The doorway-like feature survived the translation of the church to Ferrybridge, but in its present form it is totally mute as regards its original purpose. There are two similar doorway-like openings at the east ends of the arcades at Harewood; in their present form these seem to be 19th century, but originally they may have had some connection with the rood arrangements. Above the southern one is a tiny trefoil-headed recess (for a candle?) and a larger blocked cupboard or aumbry, which must relate to the loft in some way.

The most impressive late medieval chantry chapel to survive in a West Yorkshire church is undoubtedly the Waterton Chapel on the south side of the chancel at Methley (**113**). There has been some debate as to the date of the chapel, but it is now thought to be the 'Our Lady's Choir' recorded as being built in 1483-84. Here the arched recess which holds the tomb of Sir Robert Waterton and his wife is in the same position as the Harewood recesses, cut through the wall between chapel and chancel, but it is far more elaborate. On each face of the wall is an elaborately cusped and sub-cusped arch, with a groin-vaulted soffit between. The arches are set in square frames with panelled spandrels beneath hoodmoulds which terminate in splendid lion masks. The interior of the chapel has seen some alterations – there is now no sign of any piscina – but it retains a 15th-century screen dividing it from the nave aisle, and important contemporary glass in its east window. This glass, most of

114   115

A 15th-century tomb (114) in the Savile Chapel in Thornhill church (115).

which was originally in the east window of the medieval chancel, depicts figures of saints, heraldry, and angels who, following a medieval convention, are not only winged but are covered all over with feathers. There are more angels looking down from the panelled ceiling, but this is a recent repainting.

Another church with a chantry chapel which can be dated precisely is Thornhill, on the south side of the Calder valley. The tall west tower is a Perpendicular remodelling of an older structure whilst the eastern parts, beyond a nave of 1877, are of various 15th-century dates. The dating evidence is in the splendid display of medieval glass, which has been described as the best in northern England outside York. The Savile Chapel on the north side of the chancel was originally built by Sir Thomas Savile as a two-bay structure in 1447, as an inscription in one of its north windows tells us (115). The rather taller eastern bay is an extension of 1493; the glass in its east window, depicting the Resurrection of the Just, includes the request: 'Pray for the gude prosperity, mercy and grace of William Sayvile ... the which William Sayvile enlarged this quyer at his cost ... the which werke was finished the year 1493' (116). In the chancel itself the six-light east window has a Tree of Jesse and an inscription making a similar request on behalf of Robert Frost, vicar of Thornhill, who 'made new this window' and 'clerstoried and archyde this quyr', completing the works in 1499. The antiquary Dodsworth recorded another inscription, now lost, in a window of the south chapel stating that it had been added in 1491 by Robert Frost.

The problems of stylistic dating are highlighted when one compares the architectural features at Thornhill with the recorded dates. The east windows of chancel and chapels all look typical late 15th-century work, with panel tracery of the common local type. However, the two windows of the 1447 part of the north chapel have trefoiled ogee-headed lights under square frames, and look more like early 14th-century work. Similarly, the south chapel south windows also look earlier in style than the date Dodsworth records; they have been described as transitional in style between Decorated and Perpendicular. It has been suggested that both north and south windows were reset from the side walls of the earlier chancel. The chancel clerestory windows in contrast look almost Tudor: each has three lights with uncusped segmental-arched heads beneath a flattened segmental head; they could be adjudged 16th or even 17th-century work.

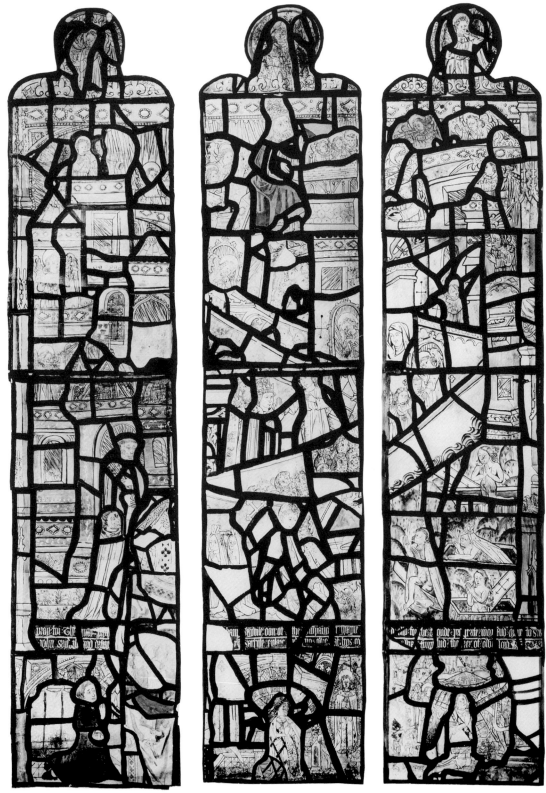

116

The east window of the Savile Chapel at Thornhill is dated 1493; it depicts the Resurrection of the Dead. These tracings of the glass were made in about 1869.

The three great town churches in West Yorkshire, at Bradford, Wakefield and Halifax, were all buildings of considerable size and status before the end of the medieval period. All underwent several phases of extension and remodelling in the 15th and early 16th centuries, and all still present the architectural historian with some problems of interpretation. Bradford and Wakefield have both been raised to cathedral status, in 1919 and 1888 respectively, and have had their eastern parts extended as a result.

At Bradford (**117**) the best surviving medieval feature is the massive western tower with heavy paired buttresses at each angle, a seven-light west window, and paired two-light belfry openings on each face below a panelled and pinnacled parapet; it is more impressive in its scale than in the quality of its detail. Documentary records show that this tower was being built over the period 1493-1508; as at Wakefield it was constructed as a free-standing structure to the west of the older nave, to which it was linked, rather clumsily, by the construction of an extra bay. Prior to this the nave aisles are said to have been built in 1408 and 1411 (reusing older arcades), the church to have been 'completed' in 1458 (presumably this refers to the eastern arm), and the nave clerestory to have been added in 1493. Unfortunately the extent of 19th and 20th-century rebuilding and extension have left little of the medieval church beyond tower, nave arcades and part of the north aisle wall.

There is also a series of dates and documentary references which one can attempt to tie in with the various phases of remodelling at Wakefield. In 1409 Archbishop Henry Bowset of York was requesting parishioners to contribute to the fabric of the new tower, dangling the carrot of four days remission from the fires of Purgatory to would-be benefactors; a bequest to the fabric of the new tower in 1420 suggests that construction was underway. The tower with its paired buttresses and double belfry openings has some similarities to the later Bradford tower, but is of more elegant

117

The eastern parts of the 15th-century parish church at Bradford, seen in this engraving, have been entirely rebuilt during the present century.

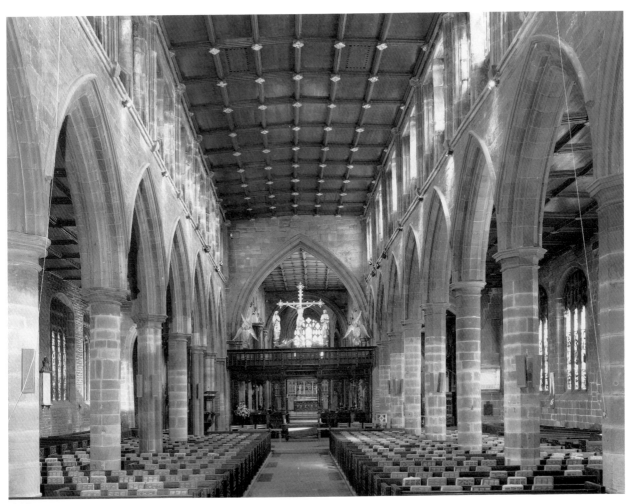

118

The parish church at Wakefield was remodelled in the 14th and 15th centuries.

proportions; the parapet is carried on moulded corbels. Behind it the lofty crocketed stone spire rises to 75m, a landmark for miles around. The fresh-looking stonework we see today is the result of Sir George Gilbert Scott's restoration of *c.* 1860. The present five-bay aisled chancel seems to have been commenced in the 1450s; a 1458 bequest implies that building was still at an early stage. The purchase of glass for the east window in 1475 may mark the completion of this phase, which was perhaps interrupted by changes in plan: the asymmetry of eight clerestory windows above an arcade of five arches hardly suggests the fulfilment of a single unified scheme. Meanwhile, the nave clerestory, with square-headed windows still reminiscent of the Decorated tradition, had been constructed (**118**). Finally the nave aisles were rebuilt to match the projection of the earlier medieval transepts, and the north and south porches added.

Halifax, the third of the 'great' medieval parish churches, is both the best preserved and in many ways the most puzzling (**119-23**). Its structural complexities suggest that, had more of the medieval fabric and features survived at Bradford and Wakefield, it might not be so easy to correlate their structures with the documentary evidence! As in the other churches, Halifax was remodelled through a number of building campaigns during the 15th and 16th centuries. The nave is said to have been built (actually rebuilt) in 1437, and the present west tower, replacing an earlier tower

119

120

121

*The oldest walling in Halifax church is on the north side (**119**); the rest is mainly 15th century, including the unusual chancel arch piers with three levels of capitals (**120**). The Holdsworth Chapel on the south side (**121**) and Rokeby Chapel on the north (**122**) were both erected in the 16th century; the oval window above the priest's door in the chancel south aisle (**123**) is a 17th-century insertion.*

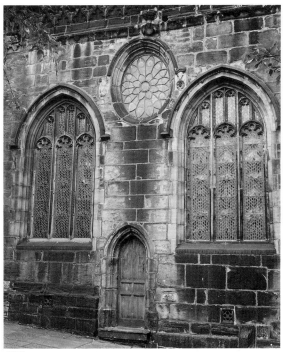

122   **123**

begun at the west end of the south aisle and probably never completed, was under construction in 1450-80. By the end of the 15th century the church had achieved the full rectangular plan, but extra space was still required; under the will of Archbishop Rokeby the Rokeby Chapel was built *c.* 1525 as an outer aisle to the north chancel chapel (**122**). The Rokeby will in fact refers to the new chapel being on the *south* side of the church, but the 1533 will of William Brig refers to 'my chauntre which I have foundid in the north part of the churche adionyng unto on Chapell lately edified and buyldid by the Reverende fader ... William Rokeby, lately the archbushope of Dublyn'.[4] It remains a puzzle why the Rokeby Chapel was built on the north rather than the south side of the church. The Holdsworth Chapel, which forms a three-bay outer south aisle to the nave (**121**), has an 18th-century inscription stating that Roger Holdsworth, then vicar, 'built this Place at his own proper Charge in 1554'. If this is correct, the chapel must be one of the latest pieces of Perpendicular architecture in the county; it bears little evidence of the degeneration or simplification of style that appears in the smaller parish churches around 1500. The buttresses on the south side of the chapel are very striking, their upper parts being in the form of tall crocketed pinnacles linked to the parapet by heavy and grotesque gargoyles in the forms of two dragons, a ram, and a man playing the bagpipes.[5] Another unusual feature, shared only by Elland, is the crypt (now a vestry) beneath the east end, its position being dictated by the slope on which the church was built.

Although many post-medieval fittings and furnishings were lost in the 19th century, the church itself has escaped major alterations or enlargement since the end of the medieval period. Halifax is arguably the finest medieval church in West Yorkshire, and one that deserves to be better known.

---

4   J.W. Clay and E.W. Crossley (eds), *Halifax Wills 1389-1544* (1904), 91

5   The south chancel chapel at South Kirkby has very similar buttresses, although here the gargoyles are rather more subdued.

124
Box pews and galleries in the late medieval church at Huddersfield (demolished 1834-35).

CHAPTER EIGHT

The Missing Centuries

The political storms and changes in religious practices which are together classed as the Reformation occupied most of the second and third quarters of the 16th century; they reduced the great wave of church building which had swept much of the country in the 15th and early 16th centuries to a trickle, if not a complete stop. There would be no large-scale construction of new buildings for the next three centuries.

This is a simple picture, and one that is only broadly correct. What it does not show is that medieval churches continued to be used, maintained, altered and occasionally extended throughout this period. In most buildings the basic shell might escape substantial external change, although features such as windows and roofs might be modified; inside a much greater transition took place, as fittings were rearranged to meet the demands of the new order. All the paraphernalia of the medieval church – the altars, chantry chapels, rood lofts and screens, ritual arrangements such as sedilia and piscina, wall paintings – disappeared, removed by either clergy or parishioners obeying Acts of Parliament, or simply through neglect and misuse. Medieval monuments, glass, and sometimes architectural features involving figure sculpture suffered heavily from either deliberate iconoclasm, simple vandalism, or the desire to realise some of the church assets (for example the brass from some monumental slabs) in a more accessible monetary form.

Whilst the trappings and trimmings of the medieval church were disappearing, their place was taken by new types of furniture and fitting. In the later 17th, 18th and early 19th centuries the increase in population, and thus of congregations, was generally catered for by the construction of galleries within the body of the church. In addition to this the introduction of fixed pewing in naves led to the interiors of churches becoming cluttered and crowded with box pews and family stalls (**124**). In terms of liturgy the Word had replaced the Sacrament, and the pulpit – often of a three-decker form, and topped by a sounding board – became the focus of the whole building. The communion table, replacing the medieval stone altar, was relatively inconspicuous.

Surviving medieval features were often concealed by plaster or stoothing; when Batley church was 'plastered and beautified' in 1740 plaster was used to convert the quatrefoil piers of the south arcade to an octagonal section, to match the north arcade. In Badsworth church a marble tablet now in the south aisle recalls the types of improvement thought desirable; it commemorates Catharine Atherton who 'bequeathed £50 to be expended in Beautifying this chancel, which after repairing the Roof, underdrawing the ceiling, sashing all the windows and raising the floor, was finished 1770'. In medieval windows the original tracery decayed and was replaced by wooden sashes, or the windows themselves might be replaced by new ones of 'pseudo-Italian' style as at Thorner.

125

126

*The nave of the medieval church at Kirkheaton (**125**) was rebuilt in 1823 (**126**) to facilitate the insertion of galleries and lofts.*

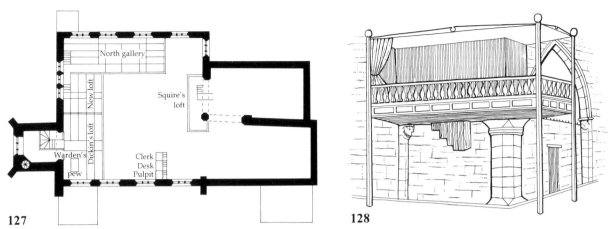

127   **128**

*A first-floor plan of Kirkheaton (**127**) shows the various galleries and lofts, including the Squire's loft (**128**; both after Legh Tolson).*

Towards the end of the period several churches were partly rebuilt or extended: no less than 804 extra sittings were gained in 1826 when the north arcade at Rothwell was taken down and the north aisle extended to admit further galleries. At Kirkheaton the nave was rebuilt in 1823 (**125, 126, 127, 128**), at Kirkburton the north aisle in 1825, and in 1826 the whole body of the church at Mirfield.

A good impression of the end results of these trends, and of the feelings they engendered in a mid-19th-century antiquary, can be gained by reading some of Sir Stephen Glynne's accounts of local churches.[1] At Bradford, in 1849, he wrote: 'it is encumbered with pews and galleries quite to an unparalleled extent'. At the west end of the nave was a 'huge gallery … there are north and south galleries besides, and another most horrible one encroaching literally over the whole chancel'. At Otley in 1860 the chancel was 'gloomy … much modernised, and has been ceiled. The greater part of it is wainscoted'. At Kippax (1862) the condition of the nave was 'thoroughly bad, having ugly pews with fusty green baize linings' and in 1863 he found the rebuilt church body at Mirfield 'hideous' and 'scarce worthy of notice. The interior is as little like a church as possible, with flat ceiling, staring ugly windows, lop-sided gallery west and north, and pews occupying the central space quite up to the altar'.

Such was the Victorian reaction to all this that, in the later 19th century, church after church was restored to an idealised medieval form, as we shall see in the next chapter. The evidences of the 'missing three centuries', in terms of both architectural features and church fittings, were ruthlessly swept away. It is only by a study of old illustrations and plans, reading accounts such as Glynne's, and carefully examining the few features that do survive, that one realises the extent to which churches were altered in the long period between the Dissolution of the monasteries, and the accession of Queen Victoria.

In the first century or so of this period, the little church building that was carried out seems frequently to have been very conservative in tradition, retaining Gothic features. For this reason it is often difficult to recognise post-medieval work when it does survive. Some of the plainer

---

1 The following quotations are taken from S. Glynne, 'Notes on Yorkshire churches', *Yorkshire Archaeological Journal* 14 (1898) – Bradford; and S. Glynne, 'Notes on Yorkshire churches', *Yorkshire Archaeological Journal* 24 (1917) – Otley, Kippax and Mirfield.

129   **130**

Heptonstall (129) was remodelled in the late 16th or 17th century; the nave arcade piers (130) probably date to that time.

'Perpendicular' church towers, such as Collingham's, which are usually assumed to be pre-Reformation might equally well be late 16th or even 17th century. It is difficult to ascertain whether the lower part of the tower at Haworth is a much-altered 15th-century piece, or part of the documented 1655 rebuilding.

Heptonstall is an even more intriguing case; in the later 16th or 17th century the medieval chapel of St Thomas Becket was remodelled, the north aisle and chancel being enlarged into a new 'north nave' and 'north chancel', and these provided with their own outer north aisle. Sir Stephen Glynne saw the building as 'a good specimen of a large rude mountain church of the West Riding' and thought that the whole structure was 'of the rough Perpendicular work abounding in the district'.[2] A closer inspection shows that some of its architectural features do not fit happily into the local range of 15th and early 16th-century motifs. The monolithic piers of the nave arcades have raised discs and squares on the abaci, whilst the east window of the north chancel has its frame decorated with strange ball-like mouldings. It is details like this, sometimes bringing in hints of Classical forms and sometimes harking back to earlier medieval periods, that suggest we are looking at post-medieval Gothic work, possibly of the late 16th or early 17th century (**129, 130**).

There is one church in West Yorkshire which, since it is neither a medieval structure nor stands on a medieval site, does not really qualify for inclusion in this book, but must be mentioned here. This is St John's in New Briggate, Leeds, founded by cloth merchant John Harrison and built

---

2   S. Glynne, *Yorkshire Archaeological Journal* 24 (1917), 315-16

131

St John's, Leeds, appears largely medieval but was in fact erected in 1632-34.

in 1632-34. In both external appearance and in the overall form of many of its features it is a medieval church adrift from its period, more so now that it has lost the typically Jacobean south porch with strapwork decoration shown on old prints (**131**). The square-headed windows with cusped tops to the lights, the stepped buttresses and embattled parapets, the west tower and the traceried windows in the east end all look like the products of the 14th and 15th centuries. Only the plan (a rectangle divided by a single longitudinal seven-bay arcade) and a variety of minor architectural details and mouldings (as at Heptonstall) point to the building as being contemporary with its splendid woodwork and fittings, which together make it a structure of national importance.

Nowhere else does post-medieval Gothic work occur on such a scale. At Emley the north chancel aisle was extended eastwards to serve as a burial chapel for the Assheton family; its east window has a '1632' inscription on its lintel. At Bradford the Bolling Chapel is said to have been built in 1615; the pair of buttresses and window that have survived the mid-20th-century alterations both have the look of 'late Perp.' work familiar in other churches. Elsewhere other medieval churches were being modified to suit new requirements: at Halifax we read of the conversion of the crypt to a library, the sum of four shillings being paid for 'dressing both Revestry and carrying out the bones'.[3]

The main structural alteration made to virtually every church in this period was, as already mentioned, the insertion of galleries. A few may have been of 16th-century date,[4] but the majority

---

3   W.R. Barnes and I.M. Longbotham, *Halifax Parish Church* (n.d.), 17

4   Glynne describes the nave galleries in old St Peter's church in Leeds as 'ancient'.

83

132
Galleries in the aisles at Dewsbury.

were introduced in the 18th and early 19th centuries. Many can be dated from surviving faculties: at Bradford in the aisles (1786) and across the chancel arch (1797); at Elland in 1725-26 with a new north gallery in 1802 and a south chancel gallery in 1805; at Heptonstall 'north and south lofts' as early as 1617 and a 'singing loft' in the north chancel in 1720; at Kirkburton in 1770 and 1780; at Otley a west gallery in 1757 and an east nave gallery, running right through the transepts, in 1793. All these have gone; the clues to their former presence are found in 19th-century patching and repair of nave arcade piers, to which the galleries were fixed, and in the remains of the doorways which gave access to galleries within towers. The majority of medieval tower stairs in the county now have a blocked doorway at the former gallery level; frequently this is visible from the tower itself only as a patched area of masonry, but from the stair the form of the opening (often roughly arched, and clearly hacked through the medieval masonry) can be seen more clearly.

There are one or two instances in which nave arcades were rebuilt with higher and wider arches to permit the insertion of galleries. This happened at Rothwell in 1826, although the arcade there was restored to its medieval form in 1873. At South Kirkby the present nave arcades are of only two bays; their architectural features are early 13th century, but the arches are unusually lofty and broad (**133**). When one looks closely it can be seen that the curves of the individual voussoirs do not quite conform to the present outline of the arch. The explanation would seem to be that three

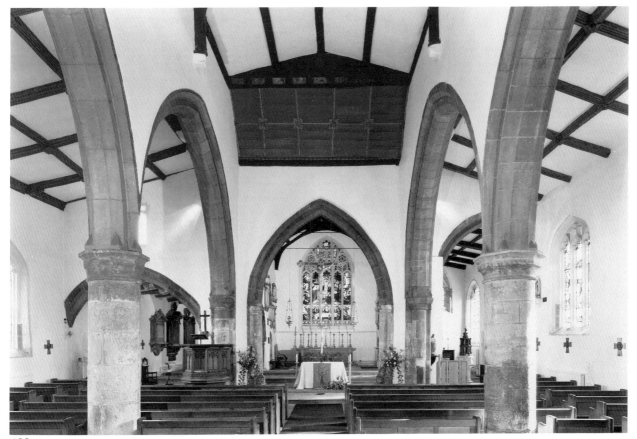

133

134

135

*The nave arcades at South Kirkby (**133**) may have been rebuilt to take galleries like those at Dewsbury. Such galleries required additional lighting, as provided by the 17th-century stepped gable windows at Heptonstall (**134**) and Elland (**135**).*

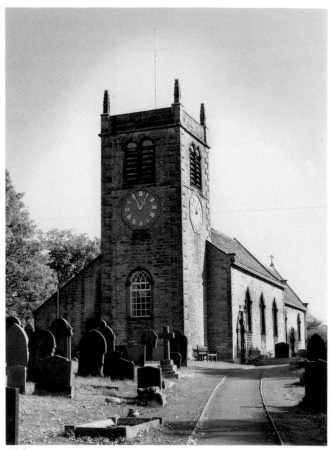

136

137

*Addingham church (**136**) was remodelled in the 1750s; its south doorway was furnished with a Gibbs surround (**137**).*

smaller arches (and the walls above) have been taken down and reconstructed, using the old materials, as two. The extra height gained by this, and by the resetting of the aisle roofs at a higher level, allowed the construction of galleries. Further evidence of this can be seen externally in that the clerestory walls lack the embattled parapets and pinnacles of the rest of the church; the only windows are square-headed mullioned ones close to the west end, which look more 17th or 18th century than medieval. The nave arcades at Sandal Magna seem to have been reconstructed at around the same time, although here the arches may simply have been heightened rather than reduced in number. The unusually lofty arcades at Bramham also provoke speculation as to whether the same thing has occurred here.

Galleries required extra light. In a number of churches this was provided by the construction of gables with large mullioned and transomed windows, raised on top of the aisle or clerestory walls. The only one to survive is that above the outer north arcade of the ruined church at Heptonstall (**134**); this has a stepped window, of a type familiar in early 17th-century houses, with quite ornate hoodmould stops. There was a similar gable and window above the south arcade, taken down *c.* 1900, and also, as Glynne tells us, 'some small quasi-clerestory windows over the central arcade, of like character'.[5] Old drawings of Elland church show a similar gable with a large window raised

---

5   S. Glynne, *Yorkshire Archaeological Journal* 24 (1917), 315-16

on the south aisle wall east of the porch (**135**); there were others at Halifax and probably also at Bingley and Birstall. An old illustration of Otley church shows small gabled dormers on the nave roof.

The Classical style eventually began to make its appearance in West Yorkshire churches in the 18th century. At Bingley in 1739 the tower received a new belfry that is still recognisably Gothic, but the chancel chapels and south aisle remodelled at about the same time seem to have had quasi-Classical angle pilasters. The tower of St Giles, Pontefract, was rebuilt to a wholly Classical design in 1707; structural failure prompted a second rebuilding in 1790-91 to the designs of a Mr Atkinson.

In 1727 Sir George Tempest of Tong Hall rebuilt the village's small 12th-century church as a building with a south elevation that is wholly Classical in detail, although the church is still of medieval proportions and plan. On the north the aisle windows revert to the common late Perpendicular or Tudor form with round-arched lights within a square frame. Inside, the arcade piers are Tuscan but the round arches double-chamfered in a tradition that was now five centuries old. The building is discussed in more detail in Chapter 12. The south aspect of Addingham church is very reminiscent of Tong, although this time there are rusticated quoins and Gibbs surrounds to the doorways. Addingham is a remodelling rather than a rebuilding (the date of 1757 appears along with the churchwardens' names on a tower string-course), and here the north aisle is genuine 15th-

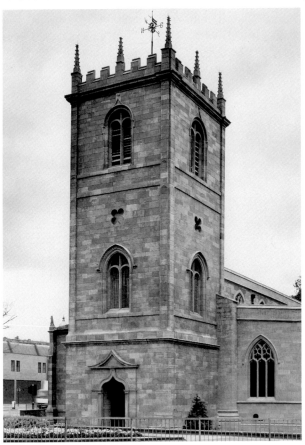 

138   **139**

*The west tower at Dewsbury (**138**) is a Gothic Revival structure of c. 1765. The doorways (**139**) have ogee-shaped arches.*

century work (136, 137). The interior of Tong remains much as it was when Sir George Tempest completed his work, although the Tempest pew, which had its own fireplace, has been reduced in height. It was now the family pew that demonstrated the presence of the local lord, rather than his chantry chapel. Addingham also retains some good 18th-century fittings including the font and west gallery.

In 1770 Anthony Crossley rebuilt the body of Todmorden chapel at a cost of £605. He retained the base of a late medieval or sub-medieval west tower, and probably some walling of a north aisle, but otherwise his building was much more akin to a nonconformist 'preaching box' chapel than to a medieval nave-and-chancel church. The six-bay south elevation demonstrates the original internal arrangements: in the centre are two tall round-arched windows, between which the pulpit stood with its back to the wall. The doorways are in the second and fifth bays, opening under galleries which ran round the west, north and east walls; in the end bays vertical pairs of Venetian windows lit the gallery and the under-gallery space. Similar symmetrical south facades are seen in two of West Yorkshire's wholly 18th-century churches, Sowerby (1763-66) and Rastrick (1796-98).

In the mid-18th century came the beginnings of the Gothic Revival with the conscious reintroduction of medieval motif. Archbishop Drummond's 1769 additions to Bishopthorpe Palace at York are in this style. Its first appearance in church architecture in West Yorkshire is in the tower and north aisle at Dewsbury, now thought to date from *c.* 1765 and to have been designed by John Carr (138). Some of the features here such as the pilaster-like angle buttresses and the little concave-sided pediments over the west and north doors are more Classical than Gothic in origin

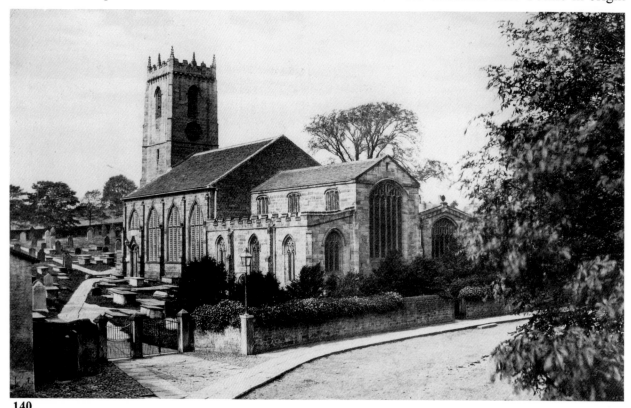

140
The 1777 nave at Thornhill, shown above, was replaced a century later by one in the 14th-century Decorated style, specifically because this style was otherwise unrepresented in the church.

(139); the ogee door arches, panelling on the pilasters and the quatrefoil panel over the west window are more typical of the Gothic Revival (or Gothick style as it is sometimes termed), but the windows with their odd tracery[6] owe more to the local tradition of Gothic survival (or post-medieval Gothic). Their closest parallels are in the surviving window of the Bolling Chapel at Bradford, and some of the windows at Heptonstall. The Victorians were not impressed by Carr's tower and aisles at Dewsbury: even Joseph Morris, writing in 1913, could dismiss them as 'rebuilt in 1767 – with what result is easily imagined';[7] we can be thankful that funds did not permit the planned replacement of the 18th-century work to extend beyond the south aisle.

An old photograph of Thornhill church before the 1877 restoration shows the 1777 nave as built in a style reminiscent of the odd Gothic-Classical mix at Dewsbury; might Carr have been responsible for this as well (140)? It is a tall and broad rectangle, obviously containing galleries. Buttresses with gabled off-sets divide the south wall into four bays, each with a large ogee-headed window with mullions and a transom; in the westernmost bay the window has its sill raised to allow for an arched doorway in an ogee-headed panel beneath. Set over the doorway is the date stone, with vicar and churchwardens' names, which now lies in the churchyard at the foot of the south aisle wall of Street's 1877 nave.

Traces of the same 18th-century Gothic style are seen in the north aisle buttresses at Wakefield, with their ogee gablets. The south elevation of both nave aisle and chancel chapel had been remodelled in 1725, to erase the irregularities caused by the piecemeal development of the medieval building: up to this date the south chapel wall seems to have incorporated the remains of the 12th-century south transept. It was a desire of the period to introduce order and symmetry. The 1725 window tracery seems to have been similar to that in Carr's aisles at Dewsbury.

John Carr did not work purely in the Gothic Revival. His most sumptuous church is at Horbury, built in 1791-93 at a cost of £8,000 on the site of a medieval building, the only visible evidence of which is a pair of medieval cross slabs. Carr built it, as Bishop Fleming is said to have built Crofton, as a tribute to his native village. It is a spectacular Classical church with an Ionic portico and a fine west tower topped by a rotunda of columns and a spire.

There are other notable 18th-century churches in West Yorkshire such as Holy Trinity in Leeds (1721-27) and St John in Wakefield (1791-95), but they do not stand on medieval sites and hence cannot qualify for a description here. Neither can the dozens of churches built in the first, pre-Victorian part of the 19th century, mostly in and around the industrial towns. The majority of these were in what was termed the 'lancet' style: a simple and unscholarly Gothic, favoured by the Church Commissioners. Some architects continued to build in the Classical style, although this was more popular for nonconformist buildings. The rediscovery of medieval church architecture, as opposed to the use of Gothic trimmings on a preaching box church, had yet to come.

---

6   Lights with heads round-arched both in the intrados and extrados, beyond which the mullions are carried straight up to join the curve of the arch.

7   J.E. Morris, *Little Guide to the West Riding of Yorkshire* (1923, 2nd ed.)

141
All Souls, Haley Hill, Halifax, a Gothic church built by Scott in 1856-59.

CHAPTER NINE

Medieval Revival

The story of the Victorian return to the medieval style in church buildings, furnishings and monuments is a long and complicated one, and is here considered only as far as it affects the medieval churches in the county. It is an important chapter in their story, as so many of the features we see today are a consequence of this period. An early 19th-century visitor would have seen many of the churches as having a decidedly less 'medieval' appearance, in terms of window forms, pitch of roofs and the treatment of their interiors, than they do today.

As we have seen, the Gothic style reappeared in the church architecture of the later 18th century, and became dominant within 50 years. The revival of the style was accompanied by a growing interest in medieval architecture. It was the architect Rickman (one of whose projects was to mass produce prefabricated Gothic churches made out of cast iron) who was the first to recognise a number of English churches as being of pre-Norman date; he published a number of formative books including his *Attempt to Discriminate the Styles of Architecture in England, from the Conquest to the Reformation* (1819). It was Rickman who coined the popular names of the three divisions of English Gothic: 'Early English', 'Decorated' and 'Perpendicular'. He and his contemporaries studied medieval buildings and adopted their style whilst considering their plan forms and fittings as something of the past, unsuitable for contemporary modes of worship. However in the mid-19th century a new wave of artists and architects saw the revival of the medieval church in style, forms and fittings as their goal; their leading light was Augustus Welby Pugin (a convert to Roman Catholicism) who in 1841 published *True Principles of Pointed or Christian Architecture*; the Ecclesiological Society was formed (and still exists) to promote the medieval ideal and to encourage (or lobby) contemporary architects in its pursuit. Sir George Gilbert Scott, one of the most famous of Victorian church architects, shared their medievalising zeal; in West Yorkshire he carried out major restorations at Wakefield and Halifax, and built a number of new churches. He thought All Souls, Haley Hill in Halifax (1856-59) 'on the whole, my best church' (**141**).[1]

All of the main medieval styles of architecture reappeared in the 19th century, very much in chronological order, and with increasing scholarly concern for correctness of detail. The early Victorian enthusiasm for the Norman or Romanesque was very much confined to the 1840s as far as new buildings were concerned. In West Yorkshire it affected few medieval churches: Chantrell's restoration of the bell-cote at Adel in 1839, and Street's more careful restoration of several windows in the same church in 1879 are exceptions. Barber had the excuse of an original south door and

---

1   N. Pevsner, *The Buildings of England: Yorkshire The West Riding* (1967, 2nd ed.), 234

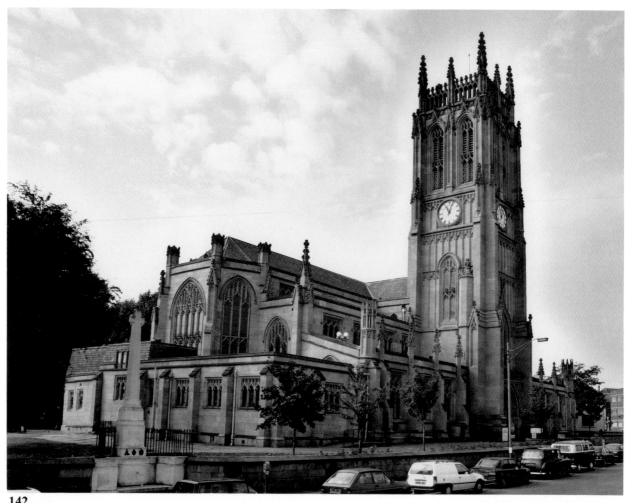

142

St Peter's, Leeds, rebuilt using a mixture of Decorated and Perpendicular motifs between 1838 and 1841.

chancel arch for his chosen style when rebuilding Hartshead church as late as 1881, but his end result here is less than happy, erasing as it did all evidence of the later medieval and post-medieval development of the building.

The Early English and the Decorated Gothic styles were the favourites of the 'High Victorian' architects of the 1850-70s, when later medieval work was often viewed as 'debased'; in restorations of this period there was a tendency for Perpendicular windows, particularly of the plainer type, to be replaced by windows in the style of a century earlier. In the later 19th century George Frederick Bodley saw the 14th century, and the transition from Decorated to Perpendicular, as the ideal, partly because the Perpendicular was 'especially an English style'. The later Victorian and early 20th-century architects handled their architecture, both in detail and in overall forms, with more liberty and imagination; Pevsner typifies Sir Charles Nicholson's 1910 extensions to Guiseley, and their relationship to the style of the older part of the church, by the phrase 'tactful freedom'.

A brief chronological survey of Victorian and more recent changes in West Yorkshire churches will show what has been gained and what has been lost. The period really began with the Leeds architect R. Dennis Chantrell, who had refurbished the transepts and crossing of the ruined All Saints at Pontefract a few years before, rebuilding St Peter's parish church, Leeds, during the years 1838 to 1841 (**142**). His church is an impressive building using a free mixture of Decorated and Perpendicular motifs that would have been more in place 60 years later; it preserves something of the form of its predecessor (it too has an outer north aisle) but nothing of its fabric. The interior is still crowded with galleries, a feature which a few years later would doubtless have drawn complaints from the Ecclesiological Society.

The restoration of Collingham church in 1840-41 was one of the last in the old Georgian tradition of 'plastering and beautifying'; the genuine medieval arcade was given elaborate stucco mouldings, as were two arched roof trusses spanning the nave, and the ribs of a wooden vault under the tower. A diversity of earlier windows were replaced by typical early 19th-century lancets (**143**); it was too early in the century for the Anglo-Saxon and medieval features in the fabric to be recognised and treated with the respect they deserved.

The changing ecclesiastical tastes of the 19th century are well seen in the various extensions and restorations at Rothwell. The 1826 extensions, already mentioned, removed the 15th-century north arcade to make way for new galleries. The chancel was rebuilt at the same time, with plain round-headed windows. In 1849 the chancel, little more than 20 years old, was 'gothicised' (**144**); then in 1873 the galleries were removed and the north arcade rebuilt so as to approximate its pre-1826 form. In 1892 the south arcade, clerestory and south aisle (**145**) were all rebuilt, but this time reproducing their original form. The end result was a church of convincing 15th-century appearance but which retains genuine medieval work only in the tower, south porch and nave roof; the last of

143
The Early English lancets at Collingham were inserted in the 1840s.

144 **145**

*The chancel (**144**) and south aisle (**145**) at Rothwell were both rebuilt in Perpendicular style during the 19th century.*

these is a rather surprising survival, and a testimony to the way in which, in both churches and secular buildings, an old roof can be retained when everything beneath it is replaced.

At Kirkthorpe in 1850-51 the church was extended by the rather strange expedient of moving both chancel arch and east end one bay to the east. Without documentary evidence this would now be a difficult building to interpret; the 19th-century stonework has decayed in places, so as to be almost indistinguishable from the medieval. Another church where sandstone ashlar has weathered to give a superficial air of antiquity is Ackworth, rebuilt, except for its tower, in 1852 after a fire. It would be interesting to know whether such features as the arcades with their quatrefoil piers, and the strange little north-east sacristy, very like that at Felkirk, reproduce what was there before.

In addition to Leeds, five other churches were completely demolished and rebuilt: at Huddersfield (1834-36) (**146, 147**), Garforth (1844), Keighley (1848), Castleford (1866) and East Ardsley (1881). Apart from a few reset monuments and old fonts, relatively few relics were preserved from the previous buildings. At Garforth a number of weathered architectural fragments lie in the churchyard; at East Ardsley a Norman doorway was reset in the new church and a Perpendicular window became a vicarage garden ornament. The bodies of the churches at Aberford (1861) (**148, 149, 150**) and Birstall (1863-70) were rebuilt, keeping the old towers; at Kirkheaton (1886-88) another fire prompted the replacement of all but the tower and north chancel chapel. At Mirfield Sir George Gilbert Scott built his new church on a new site; the medieval tower of its predecessor was preserved, but its preaching box nave which caused Sir Stephen Glynne such consternation was demolished.

Several of the other mid-century 'restorations' were destructive of medieval work: Bramham (1853), Thorner (1855), Ilkley (1861) and Hemsworth (1867) were all more in the nature of

146

147

The late medieval church at Huddersfield, with its substantial later additions converting the nave into a 'preaching box' (146), was demolished and replaced by a new building (147) in 1834-36.

148   149

The old church at Aberford, with its mutilated Norman chancel arch, can be seen before (148) and during (149) demolition in c. 1861.

remodellings. Thorner and Ilkley both had their eastern parts completely rebuilt, although at Ilkley the architect showed unusual restraint in following the very plain late Perpendicular style of the older parts of the church, so that at first glance the building looks all of one piece. By contrast, Hemsworth is externally a completely and very obviously Victorian building.

Of all the features of a church, the east window of the chancel seems to have been peculiarly vulnerable when it came to restoration or renewal; its position (directly above the altar) coupled with the Puginesque belief in Gothic as the only proper Christian style of architecture, resulted in it being one of the first features to be replaced. At Batley, a church which Joseph Morris could still call 'practically unrestored' in 1913, a traceried east window was inserted in 1856, quite out of character with the very simple fenestration which still survives in the rest of the building. Unhappier still are the obtrusive Gothic east windows which the Victorians obviously felt conscience-bound to insert in the delightful early Georgian churches at Tong and Addingham.

Although the general trend of 19th-century restoration was to return old churches to their medieval form, many had genuine medieval features destroyed, or restored out of all recognition. In 1856 when Scott rebuilt the north aisle at Barwick in Elmet he saw no need to replace the blocked north door. As late as 1881 at Hartshead a jumble of medieval, 17th and 18th-century features were erased to make way for a Romanesque remodelling which took its style from the surviving 12th-century chancel arch and south door. In general the moral crusade was aimed at the post-medieval and 'debased'; significant medieval features were retained when possible, although often much of their stonework was renewed. If one looks at the period from the point of view of an archaeologist rather than an architectural historian, the losses were far heavier.

150
The 1861 chancel arch and nave at Aberford, looking towards the west tower. For a comparable view of the previous church see above left (148).

In almost every church an underfloor central heating system was introduced. This involved the digging of broad trenches throughout the building, destroying sub-floor deposits and remains of earlier structures; it also often involved the creation of a boiler room which would entirely destroy the archaeology of a section of the building, as in the base of the tower at Ledsham. 'Finds' such as pieces of Anglo-Saxon crosses, medieval grave slabs or attractive architectural fragments might be retained and either put on display in a 'museum corner' or built into an aisle or porch wall. Despite this, in almost every case no proper record was made of the structures and stratigraphy disturbed. At Methley a trapdoor was left in the nave floor so that the footings of a 12th-century or earlier cross-wall can still be examined, but elsewhere either the barest of written mentions sufficed (as for foundations beneath the nave at Thornhill) or the features seen were completely ignored. Although the construction of heating systems was the main cause of the destruction of sub-floor deposits, it was not the only one; church floor levels were sometimes lowered in the course of improvements. A modern archaeologist would have found it very interesting to have been at hand when the floors at Bardsey were dropped 14 inches (0.35m) during the 1909-14 works there.

Much has also been lost above ground level. Whilst restorations usually aimed to restore the basic structure and architectural features of a church to its medieval form, the bones were often left bare. Prior to the 15th century, church walls were clad, internally and externally, with plaster, limewash and render. This practice had very early origins: there appear to be remains of some form of render on the west gable of the original nave at Ledsham. The exposed stonework of many church interiors, although it reveals much of archaeological interest, would never have been seen in earlier centuries. The removal and renewal of wall plaster occasioned much destruction of medieval and post-medieval paintings. In many cases these had been covered by later layers of plaster, and may have been removed without their existence ever being realised. At the priory church of Woodkirk, where rebuilding was occasioned by the collapse of the nave roof in 1831, the removal of lath and plaster disclosed extensive remains of floral decoration; the historian Norrison Scatcherd watched as 'the rude innovating hands of the workmen tore from the south wall the painted and gilded plaster unmindful of its beauty'.[2] Virtually no remains of wall paintings are visible in West Yorkshire churches today, except at Lotherton Hall Chapel and Woolley, but the plastered walls of other churches may conceal earlier decoration, although some were stripped and replastered last century. One of the more exciting recent developments in archaeology is the use of remote-sensing techniques, including forms of photography that can 'see' through plaster and detect both paintings and concealed structural features. Thus the latest technology can be applied to the study of medieval churches; as yet the vast majority of churches still await this form of examination.

To conclude with two detailed examples, it is instructive, and in some ways depressing, to chronicle the various changes the 19th and 20th centuries have wrought on West Yorkshire's two great parish churches now elevated to cathedral status.

All Saints church at Wakefield entered the 19th century as a large late medieval building, the outer walls of which had been largely refaced or rebuilt in the 1700s. In general the church had been well cared for, although decaying stonework in the tower and spire was giving cause for concern. A major restoration was decided on, and Scott, despite the questionable success of his recent 'restoration' of the Bridge Chantry, was called in. His works spanned the years from 1858 to 1874.

---

2   N. Scatcherd, cited in D. Lindstrum, *West Yorkshire: Architects and Architecture* (1978), 167

The tower and spire were the most urgent concern: the former was completely refaced and the latter rebuilt. The 18th-century windows were all replaced in a more suitable medieval style; the walls were stripped of plaster (some remains of medieval paintings were recorded before their destruction) and most of the furnishings except the chancel screen and stalls were renewed. J.T. Micklethwaite, the antiquary-cum-architect who worked alongside Scott, studied the fabric in some detail and advanced a very plausible interpretation of its complex building history.

In 1888 the parish church was raised to cathedral status, and it was soon felt that the building should be dignified and enlarged to befit its new rank . In 1901-05 a major extension was constructed at the east end, F.L. Pearson being the architect. The east walls of the old chancel and chapels were

151
Almondbury church hall, built on the north side of the parish church in 1990 and linked to it by a corridor.

99

removed, and a new eastern transept and sanctuary built in a rather more ornate and free Perpendicular style than that of the medieval building. In the course of these works, foundations thought to be of an Anglo-Saxon building were uncovered, but no proper record was made of them. The only real archaeological work that has been carried out at Wakefield came in 1974 when repair work prompted the excavation of two areas of the nave floor; more recently, a trial excavation was made before the building of the Treacy Memorial Hall, close to the north side of the church.

St Peter's church at Bradford has suffered rather more heavily than All Saints. At the beginning of the 19th century it consisted of an eight-bay aisled nave with a west tower, and a chancel with its sanctuary projecting beyond two-bay chapels. There seems to have been the same problem with decaying stonework here as at Wakefield, which may have prompted the rebuilding of the south aisle, clerestory and porch in 1833 by Leeds architect James Clark. In 1899 another local firm, T.H. & F. Healey carried out a restoration and added 'transepts' (in reality short outer aisles) to the nave. The parish church became a cathedral in 1919; the consequent remodelling came only after World War II, when major extensions designed by Sir Edward Maufe, the architect of Guildford Cathedral, were carried out over the period 1951-65. Apart from fragments of its side chapels, the medieval eastern arm was replaced by a new lantern tower, choir and eastern chapels, whilst two wings were built onto the side walls of the tower.

The new eastern arm of the cathedral is a striking piece of 20th-century architecture, especially internally, but it is perhaps arguable whether the destruction of the medieval chancel would have been permitted today; it was reportedly 'unsafe' (a common condition in old buildings under threat of demolition); all that was saved were a piscina and a few carved timbers from what appears to have been an elaborate 14th or 15th-century roof. What is more saddening is that, even in the mid-20th century, an archaeological opportunity was missed. During the digging of new foundation trenches the footings of an earlier chancel were seen. They were observed to be 'burnt', and thought to date to *c.* 1200, but it appears no proper record was made before the evidence was destroyed.

The works at Bradford underline the fact that it is the archaeological rather than the architectural aspect of church buildings which is most at risk in the 20th century. Whilst at the time of writing redundancies of church buildings are more common than major extensions, minor works that involve the disturbance and destruction of archaeological deposits still frequently take place; interiors are reordered, drainage trenches are dug around churches, floors are relaid and church halls or parish centres are built next to historic church buildings (**151, 152**). In all these activities, archaeological material is being damaged or destroyed, often unwittingly. In the 19th century the Ecclesiological Society and its like fought for the preservation of the architecture and historic fittings of English churches and cathedrals. Today it is the turn of archaeologists to raise their voices: not to object to the continuing changes which have always been part of the life of church buildings, but to ensure that proper records and investigations are made, so that the past may yield the maximum amount of information to the present.

152

*As long as they remain in use, church buildings will be adapted to cater for the current requirements of Christian ministry. The church hall, as seen here at Batley and at Almondbury (**151**), is one of the most common late 20th-century adaptations; it embodies information on religious and social perceptions in precisely the same way as the numerous chantry chapels which were erected in the 14th century.*

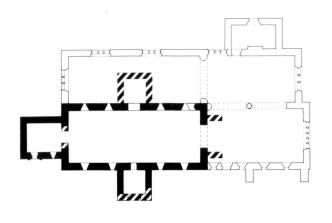

LEDSHAM *Early 8th century*

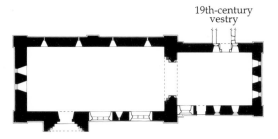

ADEL *Mid- to late 12th century*

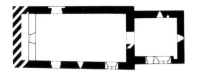

LOTHERTON *Late 12th century*

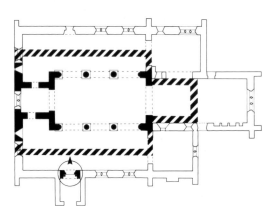

BARDSEY *End of 12th century*

153

Comparative plans of churches at specific periods: solid black indicates surviving masonry; diagonal shading indicates demolished walls (known or supposed); circles indicate repositioned features, the arrows pointing to their original locations; outlined walls mark the extent of the present church; all at a scale of 1 inch to 32 feet (1:384).

CHAPTER TEN

Church Plans

by Stuart Wrathmell

The ten plans of medieval churches in this chapter have been included to illustrate the ranges of size and form encountered in West Yorkshire. They also exemplify some of the main changes which occurred between the 8th and 16th centuries. The differences resulted not only from the varying importance of the individual churches, but also from changes in ritual and liturgical practice during the Middle Ages.

The extremes of size are marked by Lotherton, the chapel of a small 12th-century community, and Halifax, the great 15th-century parish church of a prosperous textiles town. Many of the early churches had a simple nave and chancel plan (even one decorated as elaborately as 12th-century Adel), though the two best-preserved pre-Conquest buildings (Bardsey and Ledsham) also had *porticus* or chambers attached to the sides and west end of the nave. Small, simple structures continued to be built (as at Walton in the 14th century). From Norman times, however, nave walls were frequently pierced by arcades, to give access to aisles built on one or both sides (as at Bardsey and Guiseley). So, too, were the side walls of chancels, often in the 14th and 15th centuries to make room for chantry chapels where masses could be celebrated for the souls of the departed. By the end of the 15th century a church such as Halifax could have arcades stretching from one end to the other. Many western towers seem also to have been added in the later Middle Ages.

A minor but significant theme in church planning is marked by those buildings which have a tower at the junction of nave and chancel, with transepts on their north and south sides; the best example is Crofton, a small 15th-century building erected by an important churchman in his native village. Earlier cruciform churches, such as Sandal Magna, seem to have been places of particular importance in Anglo-Saxon and Norman times.

The following plans emphasise by shading the shape of a church at a specified period, within the outlines of the present building; diagonal shading marks walling which has since been removed, but which is known or conjectured to have existed at the period in question. Circles and arrows mark doorways and windows later removed and reset elsewhere in the building. They are drawn from a number of existing sources, but incorporate some modifications as to dimensions or interpretation. The plans of Adel, Bardsey, Guiseley, Ledsham, Lotherton and Walton are after S.D. Kitson (surveyed 1920-21: Yorkshire Archaeological Society MS 1101); Crofton is after L.A.S. Butler (*Yorkshire Archaeological Journal* 62 (1990), 129); Harewood is after S.D. Kitson and L.A.S. Butler (*Yorkshire Archaeological Journal* 58 (1986), 88); Halifax is after T.W. Hanson (*The Story of Old Halifax* (Halifax 1920), 77); Sandal Magna is after J.W. Walker (*Yorkshire Archaeological Journal* 24 (1917), 21).

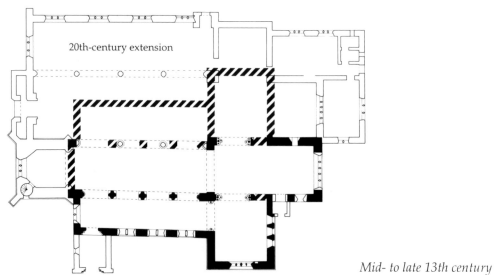

GUISELEY *Mid- to late 13th century*

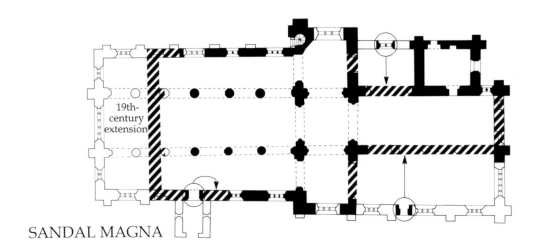

SANDAL MAGNA *Early 14th century*

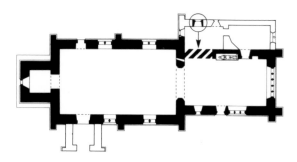

WALTON *Mid-14th century*

154

*Comparative plans of churches at specific periods: for key to shading and scale see caption to **153**.*

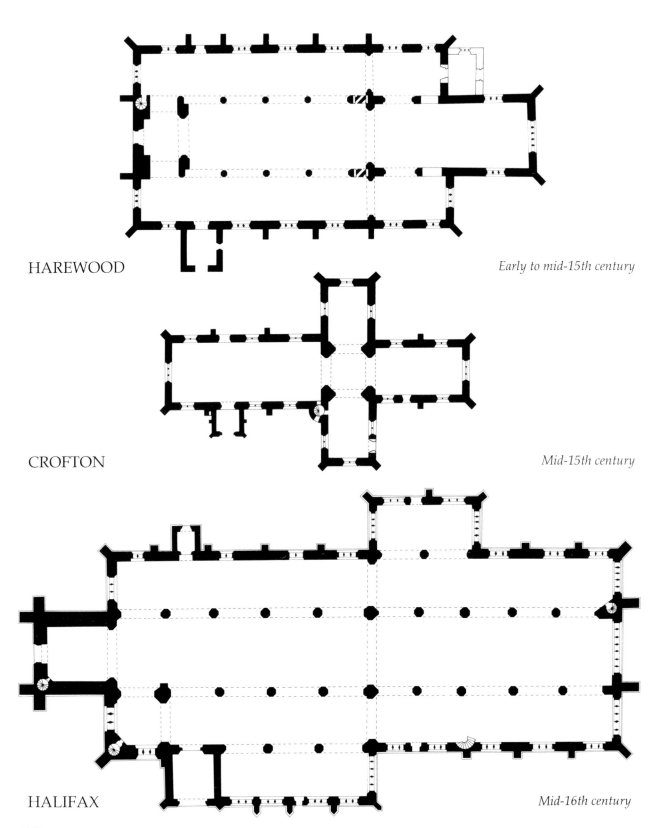

HAREWOOD   *Early to mid-15th century*

CROFTON   *Mid-15th century*

HALIFAX   *Mid-16th century*

155

Comparative plans of churches at specific periods: for key to shading and scale see caption to **153.**

105

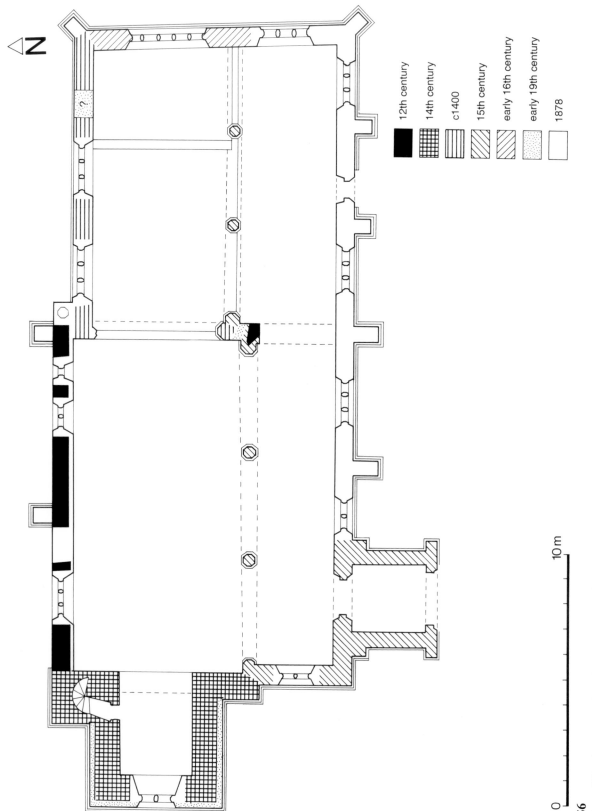

N

12th century
14th century
c1400
15th century
early 16th century
early 19th century
1878

0   10 m

156 *Plan of Featherstone church, showing the different phases of construction represented in the present building.*

CHAPTER ELEVEN

Featherstone Church: A Level 2 Investigation

The concept of different levels of investigation of a church fabric was explained in Chapter One. The following account of Featherstone church is the result of a level 2 investigation, and is typical of those carried out in the course of the Churches Survey. A level 2 examination is one in which, besides a stylistic assessment of architectural features, the fabric of the church is looked at in detail, taking special note of features such as changes in masonry, wall thickness, and the fragmentary survival of features such as blocked openings. This often gives us a very different picture of the history of the church than would the simpler 'guide-book writer's' approach; one that is nearer to the truth, but raises many awkward questions! Featherstone church, a building that has been virtually ignored in the past, is a good example of what can be achieved by the 'level 2' treatment.

Featherstone parish church is typical of a number of West Yorkshire churches in that it has attracted little antiquarian attention, and has been disregarded by a number of writers on the grounds of the relatively plain nature of its architectural features, and the degree of Victorian restoration and renewal of stonework. This attitude is exemplified by the brief descriptions of the church given in two West Riding guidebooks, those of Morris and Pevsner. Morris first:

'Featherstone has a church of no particular interest, the details of which seem wholly Perp. or Debased. Almost the single object of note, in fact, is the octagonal font ... Notice the ribbed and slabbed S porch.'[1]

Pevsner is little more enthusiastic:

'ALL SAINTS. Church of blackened stone, over-restored. Its S side faces mountainous coal-tips, its N side looks over a neighbouring estate of recent brick bungalows. The only un-Victorian-looking part is the S porch with a stone roof on three massive single-chamfered transverse arches. S aisle arcades and S chapel arcade with the standard Perp. elements ...'[2]

Neither of these accounts does the church any justice at all. As regards its surroundings, Pevsner's 'mountainous coal-tips' have largely been cleared; one can still appreciate Sir Stephen

---

1   J.E. Morris, *Little Guide to the West Riding of Yorkshire* (1923, 2nd ed.), 90

2   N. Pevsner, *Buildings of England: Yorkshire The West Riding* (1967, 2nd ed.), 198

157
Featherstone church from the south.

Glynne's 1868 comment that 'the churchyard is very pleasant, planted with trees and commanding a fine view.'[3]

The following case study is typical of those prepared for each church during the recent survey, following the usual formula of description, interpretation of the structure, and a brief record of monuments, fittings, the churchyard, and the archaeological potential of the site.

All Saints Church, Featherstone

Featherstone parish church consists of a nave with a three-bay S aisle, W tower and S porch, and a three-bay chancel with a S chapel.

Exterior

The tower has been entirely refaced in diagonally tooled squared gritstone, with the exception of the plinth and course above, and the stair projection; these show large blocks of grit, much worn. The chamfered plinth is the lower member of a former two-part plinth (cf. the adjacent buttress at the W end of the aisle and the stair turret), the moulded upper member of which was

---

3   S. Glynne, 'Church notes', *Yorkshire Archaeological Journal* 26 (1922), 166

158

159

160

161

*The ringing chamber and belfry openings (**158**); three-light (**159**) and single light (**160**) windows in the north wall of the nave; masonry in north wall of chancel marking the position of a former vestry or sacristy (**161**).*

removed when the tower was reclad in the C19; the later facing is flush with the face of the centre portion of the old plinth. The tower itself has no buttresses or set-backs. The two-light W window is wholly late C19. At the NE corner a rectangular projecting stair turret has a chamfered set-back at mid-height, two almost square windows, and a pent slab roof. The ringing chamber has square-headed windows on N, W and S; the latter shows its original ogee(?) head, much worn, set back behind the C19 recladding (**158**). The belfry openings have double-chamfered arches, and are each of two cinquefoil-headed lights divided by a mullion which continues up to the apex of the arch. The mullions and cusped heads of the lights appear to be of magnesian limestone. There is a moulded string-course below the embattled parapet.

The N wall of the nave shows a variety of fabric types; at the base are two courses of large diagonally tooled blocks, perhaps C19 work replacing an original plinth. Above are smaller courses of roughly squared stone with horizontal tooling, perhaps early medieval work recut; this fabric appears to correlate with an early NW quoin (just short of the present W end of the wall) of fairly small alternate blocks, extending up to a set-back (at the W end of the wall only) which marks the upper limit of the horizontally tooled stone. The upper third of the wall is of large squared gritstone blocks, apparently of later medieval date. Areas of diagonally tooled squared gritstone are clearly associated with the insertion of the three windows in the wall. There are two large stepped buttresses, near the centre and at the E end of the wall. The position of a former N door, just W of the central buttress, is marked by a patch of the same type of fabric as in the lowest two courses. To the W of the buttress is a square-headed window of three lights (**159**) with shallow gabled heads, and to the E a similar one of two lights; these appear wholly C19. Near the E end of the wall is a single-light window with a double-chamfered surround (**160**); its inner order has a flattened Tudor arch, and looks pre-C19 in part. The wall is capped by a moulded string and an embattled moulded parapet, all restoration. The S wall of the nave (**157**), above the aisle roof, shows old squared masonry (without any sign of clerestory openings) below a restored embattled parapet. A short length of the W wall of the nave is exposed immediately S of the tower, and has a broad stepped buttress.

The external walls of the S aisle show two quite different fabric types. The W wall and S wall W of the porch are of smallish squared stone with a distinctive 'pecked' tooling; E of the porch the S wall is of diagonally tooled squared gritstone, the result of late C19 rebuilding or refacing. The W wall has a two-part plinth at a slightly lower level than the plinth of the adjacent buttress. The upper member is chamfered; the N part of the lower member is square and the S part chamfered. The square-headed W window of the aisle is of two trefoil-headed lights, and seems completely C19. The rebuilt or refaced section of the S wall E of the porch has a two-part plinth with a moulded upper member, and stepped buttresses between the bays and at the E end. The centre bay has a square-headed window of two trefoil-headed lights and the E bay a plain three-light mullioned window. This section of the wall, unlike that W of the porch, has a hollow-chamfered off-set at the base of the parapet (continuous the whole length of the aisle, although only the section W of the porch looks old) which has a crenellated moulded coping.

The side walls of the porch (**162**) are of old squared gritstone; the S wall has either been rebuilt or refaced. The porch has a chamfered plinth, and buttresses with moulded tops at each end of each side wall. The outer arch has a continuous hollow chamfer, very worn; the S angles are capped by renewed crocketed pinnacles. Each side wall has an oversailing parapet with a moulded coping, carried on two or three shallow corbel-like features incorporating drainage spouts.

The N wall of the chancel has a single chamfered plinth; the wall is of old squared gritstone, with three lower courses just below the moulded string at the base of the crenellated and moulded parapet. In the centre and W bays (there is no external bay division) are square-headed windows each of three gable-headed lights, C19 and very like those in the N wall of the nave; an area of later stonework above the head of each suggests that they replaced pre-C19 windows with taller heads of a different type. The lower third of the wall-face of the E bay is slightly recessed, and contains a blocked square-headed door (161). Above this, two-thirds of the way up the wall, is a projecting moulded course (much cemented over); these features appear to be connected with a removed sacristy or vestry.

The E wall of the chancel has an old moulded plinth, and a stepped diagonal buttress (C19?) at the NE corner. The upper half of the wall is rendered; the lower part shows old squared gritstone, except for a refaced area above window sill level at the N end (163). The E window is of five lights (164), under a segmental-arched head and a moulded hood with turned-back ends; the surround and hood are heavily cemented. Below a transom at little more than mid-height each light has a Tudor-arched head and sunk spandrels; above the transom the sub-lights have pointed heads, stepped to follow the curve of the arch; the E window of the S chapel at Normanton is very similar. Above and to the left of the window the return of a moulded string below the parapet on the S of the chancel survives, just below the coping of the adjacent chapel roof, implying either that the chapel is an addition or that its roof-line has been changed.

162
The south porch, mainly of the 15th century.

111

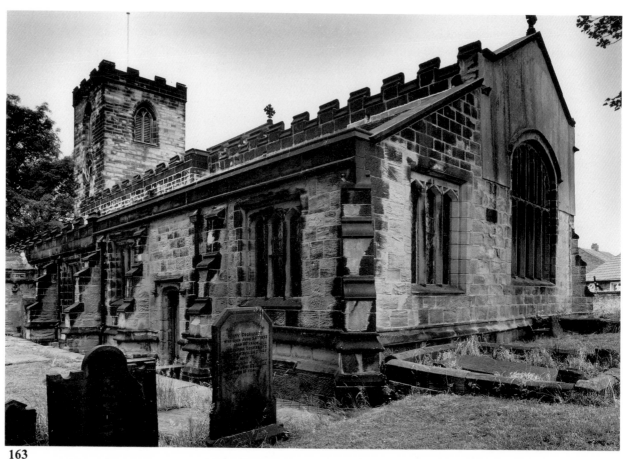

163

The south chapel and the east wall of the chancel.

The external walls of the S chapel are of the same diagonally tooled C19 gritstone as the E part of the nave S aisle, except for a patch of older masonry at the N end of the E wall (which courses in with the chancel E end). The S wall has a two-part moulded plinth, stepping up in level in the E bay; there are stepped buttresses between the bays and set diagonally at the SE corner. The central bay has a priest's door with flattened Tudor arch with a continuous hollow chamfer, and a hoodmould with turned-back ends; it is difficult to say whether the arch is old, or badly weathered C19 work. The end bays of the S wall have square-headed windows of three lights with flattened Tudor arches; the E window is of the same type (**163**).

Interior

The internal walls of the tower are of large gritstone blocks with C19 vertical tooling (continued across the infill of the sockets for gallery timbers, in the side walls). The pointed tower arch is of plain square section (very like the rear arch of the W window) and has probably been altered at some post-medieval date; it appears (see below) to be an insertion in an older wall. On the N is a chamfered shoulder-arched doorway to the stair turret. The rear arch of the W window is cut straight through the wall, without any splay, and looks post-medieval as well. The floor of the ringing chamber is carried on a projecting moulded course, much damaged, on the N and S walls.

The newel stair in the NE turret is capped by a corbelled vault, and has a second shoulder-arched doorway opening into the ringing chamber. The E wall of the chamber has a blocked square-headed loop, apparently opening behind the nave roof, with lower down two sockets for axial timbers and what appears to be a roughly infilled cavity near the N end. Access to the belfry is by ladder.

The W wall of the nave shows several puzzling features; in its masonry are areas of large but rather irregularly shaped 'long' blocks, not seen anywhere else in the church. Immediately above the apex of the tower arch are what appears to be the head and top of the N jamb of a square-headed opening largely cut away by the arch. At about the same level there are projecting areas of masonry at each end of the wall; that on the N shows a former steeply pitched roof-line which correlates with that visible on the W wall of the chancel.

The three-bay S arcade has double-chamfered pointed arches with broach stops (some cut back), resting on octagonal piers and semi-octagonal responds; these have moulded capitals (that of the W respond renewed). The W respond and W pier have swept bases, the E pier a renewed stepped base, and the E respond no base at all. The thinner upper courses of the wall above the arcade suggest that it has been heightened. The W respond seems to have been cut out of a thicker piece of wall, which has a butt-joint with the W wall of the aisle. The nave N wall seems to have been entirely refaced internally, relatively recently, and shows no features of interest.

The porch encloses the S door, which has a much worn double-chamfered pointed arch without any imposts. The porch has stone benches which at their N ends appear to be built up against the plinth of the aisle wall – however, the upper parts of the porch walls are coursed in with the aisle. The slab roof is carried on three double-chamfered, two-centred arches.

The chancel is entered under a pointed arch of two hollow-chamfered orders on semi-octagonal responds with capitals showing the same moulding as those of the nave arcade piers (**165**); on the W side of the wall the mouldings are carried back along the wall face, and there is a blocked squint (shown open on a 1904 plan kept in the vicarage) on the S, allowing a view of the S chapel

164   **165**

*The east window (**164**) and the chancel arch (**165**).*

166   **167**

A blocked doorway in the north wall of the chancel (166), and the chancel's late medieval ceiling (167).

altar. The responds have swept bases. The E face of the wall (i.e. towards the chancel) shows an earlier roof-line, this continues down beyond the line of the arcade on the S, proving that it represents a former E gable of the nave rather than a roof raggle for an earlier chancel roof. The three-bay arcade to the chapel has double-chamfered arches on octagonal piers with moulded capitals again similar to those of the nave arcade, although the piers are taller and the arches narrower. The E arch dies into the E wall, without any respond. The relationship between the W arch and the chancel arch respond suggests that the latter is of earlier construction. Near the E end of the N wall of the chancel is a blocked doorway with a Tudor-arched head (**166**), and an aumbry, any detail of which is obscured by a modern locker built into it.

The S and E walls of the S chapel are mostly of C19 squared gritstone; the break between medieval and C19 fabric in the E wall comes in much the same position as on the external wall face, suggesting that the wall has been rebuilt rather than refaced. The priest's door on the S has a plain square-headed rear arch. The chapel has an old double-chamfered pointed arch on the W, opening into the nave aisle; the adjacent angle of masonry appears to be the SE corner of an earlier aisleless nave, although the character of the quoins is partly obscured by refacing; they seem fairly small, as at the NW corner (see exterior description).

The roofs of the nave (a three-bay king-post roof with traceried openwork panels), S aisle and S chapel are all later C19. The chancel however has a well-preserved C15 or early C16 panelled ceiling (**167**). It is of three bays, with slightly cambered moulded tie-beams; the wall-posts and arch braces look like later additions. Each bay is divided into 18 panels (3 along and 6 across) by moulded timbers; there are gilded bosses at the intersections of the timbers and on the faces of the tie-beams, mostly of flower motifs but with shields bearing 'M' and 'IHC' monograms over the E bay, and several grotesque heads in the centre and W bays.

114

Interpretation

The church shows evidence for a number of building phases, although C19 refacing and restoration have obviously obscured many points. The oldest fabric is seen in the N wall of the nave and again at its SE corner; this may well be C12, although very little in the way of datable features survives. At the W end, the relationship between the original NW quoins and the present W wall of the nave is puzzling; the W end seems to have been rebuilt on a line immediately W of the quoins, at a relatively early date. The rebuilding might have been associated with the addition of a tower or belfry; the evidence of a steeply pitched roof with low eaves on the nave end walls is probably associated with the first phase.

The odd break between the two sections of the lower plinth member at the W end of the S aisle suggests the possibility of an earlier narrower aisle here, although the eaves level of the original nave hardly seems high enough to allow one. (A limited excavation inside the aisle in February 1989 exposed the footings of this wall, which seemed all of one build.)

Later medieval remodelling seems to have taken place in a number of phases. The little that survives of original architectural detail in the tower (notably the shoulder-arched doorways to the stair) points to a C14 rather than a C15 date. The hollow chamfers of the chancel arch suggest that this was renewed *c.* 1400; the chancel may have been rebuilt at the same time, along with a NE sacristy that may have been vaulted.

The addition of the nave S aisle (and porch) probably followed soon after: two of the S aisle windows, although C19 in their present form, are C14 rather than C15 in style; Sir Stephen Glynne refers to a 'square-headed Edwardian window of two lights' at the W end of the aisle.[4] The arches of the chancel arcade, 'lighter and loftier' (Glynne) than those of the nave arcade, are probably later C15 work. The capitals of chancel arch and both arcades are all very similar (what Pevsner calls 'standard Perp. elements'): it is difficult to be sure of the order of construction, except that the chancel arcade is later than the chancel arch.

A final medieval phase, probably in the early C16, is indicated by the slightly oblique alignment of the E wall of chancel and S chapel, and the absence of any E respond to the S arcade. Together these suggest a rebuilding of the E end, which presumably took place at the same time that the chancel walls were heightened and the present panelled ceiling was constructed. The simple panel tracery of the E window is very similar to that of the E window of the S chapel at Normanton, described as 'newe' in a 1519 will; the uncusped heads of the lower range of lights are also paralleled in the E window at Wragby (1533). The external walls of the chapel, which have windows more C16 than C15 in style, may have been rebuilt at the same time as well. The windows on the N side of the church, three in the nave and two in the chancel, if correctly restored, all look of this date as well.

Post-medieval alterations to the fabric have been relatively minor. The sacristy on the N side of the chancel was demolished at some date, its function being superseded by a vestry in the S chancel chapel, no longer needed as a Lady chapel or chantry. A plain three-light mullioned window in the S aisle looks C17 or even early C18 in style. At some stage the tower was remodelled, and all the dressed stonework of the tower arch cut away, possibly when a gallery was inserted. The external cladding of the tower may be early C19.

---

4   S. Glynne, 'Church notes', *Yorkshire Archaeological Journal* 26 (1922), 166

Sir Stephen Glynne's account provides a good description of the church prior to the major 1878 restoration. He mentions a number of features not visible today. Apart from the W window of the aisle, all the nave windows had 'been mutilated' (converted to sashes?). The nave had a 'flat panelled roof' (perhaps of the same date as that surviving over the chancel). In the E wall of the chancel were 'two aumbryes'; there was a niche over the outer arch of the porch. On the N of the nave was 'a closed doorway in the form of a flattened trefoil'. The W window was 'mutilated'. The interior of the church was 'unimproved' with a W gallery containing an organ.

Sepulchral Monuments

There are no medieval monuments. On the chancel floor are several C18 ledger stones; there are said to be others, including some C17 ones – the graves of a Roundhead and Cavalier are said to lie on either side of the altar – concealed by the sanctuary carpet. At the E end of the nave is a slab to Philip Cramlington 1699. On the N wall of the nave are two wall monuments from the first half of the C19, and there is a pedimented tablet to Rev. Christopher Driffield 1788 on the N wall of the chancel above the blocked vestry door.

Fittings and Furnishings

The font at the W end of the S aisle is of magnesian limestone, and octagonal; the bowl has carved shields (two in relief, one incised) on three sides and an inscription on the N: 'Iohes de Baghill + Katerina uxsor eius'. John de Baghill died in 1451; the font is said to have been brought here from Pontefract in the Civil War.

The bells were rehung in new frames in 1977; a section of the old frame, with the inscription 'MRLS 1682' has been set into the W wall of the nave to the S of the tower arch. The bells are inscribed:

(1)   + Sci Jacobi Huius

(2)   Sancti Petri Apoli Huius

(3)   + In Multis Annis Resonet Campana Johannis +[5]

A sheet of information on the bells, framed and hung on the W wall of the nave, states that the Tenor bell is of C15 date and by John Danyell of London, and that the 2nd and Treble are C16 from a Nottingham foundry.

The Churchyard

The churchyard is rectangular in plan, with its longer axis E-W; the church stands towards its NE corner. The S and W walls are *c.* 1m high, with a low arched coping, and look late C18 or early C19 in date; there are some obviously reused blocks, including one with possible traces of carving, in the internal face of the wall near the SW corner. The N and E walls have a flat

---

5   Inscriptions from J.E. Poppleton, 'Notes on the bells of the ancient churches of the West Riding of Yorkshire', *Yorkshire Archaeological Journal* 16 (1901), 46-83

coping and look later C19. Seven metres SW of the S porch is a magnesian limestone cross shaft with chamfered corners and broach stops at the base; it rests in a socket stone or base which is virtually buried. The shaft now stands to *c.* 1.5m high, and has the remains of a fitting, probably for a sundial, at the top. It is locally called 'The Devil's Stone'. The southern parts of the churchyard have been partly cleared of monuments, but several recumbent slabs of the period 1680-1725 survive, with quite ornate incised designs in a distinctive vernacular style. Four metres SW of the priest's door is an armorial slab, in the same style, to John Potter 1694.

Archaeological Potential

Heating grilles show that there is an underfloor system in the nave, and there is an underfloor heating chamber beneath the W part of the chancel. Most of the floors are of relatively recent stone slabs, with boarded areas beneath the pews and choir stalls. Outside, there is a sunk tiled area adjacent to the S, E and W walls, and a sunk area of bare soil alongside the N wall.

Site visit 15.2.88

168
The 18th-century fittings in Tong church.

CHAPTER TWELVE

Tong Church: A Level 3 Investigation

by Andrew Swann

A level 3 study is one in which archaeologists are able to examine and record all parts of a church fabric, above and below ground. Opportunities for this type of study occur rarely, and usually only when major structural works are being carried out; as well as the Wharram Percy project mentioned in the first chapter, investigations of this type have been possible at Hickleton (South Yorkshire) and Kellington (North Yorkshire), both churches which were seriously affected by mining subsidence. Within West Yorkshire the nearest approach to a full level 3 investigation has been at Tong, where both the sub-floor remains of the medieval church and the fabric of its 18th-century successor were examined in detail.

Introduction

The church of St James, Tong (SE 2193 3054) lies in the village of Tong, in the medieval parish of Birstall. The present building was erected in the early part of the 18th century by Sir George Tempest; it was consecrated in the year 1727, and has been little altered since. In the early 1960s it became apparent that damp was causing damage to the wooden fittings and the structure. Despite remedial work the problem continued, and a survey carried out in 1978 showed that many of the fine 18th-century furnishings and fittings were at risk (**168**). Early in 1979 a proposal was made to remove the furnishings, floor boards, and paved surfaces throughout, and to lay down a consolidated damp course. To facilitate this, a minimum of 400mm of deposits were required to be removed below the floor level. The proposed measures meant that any archaeological remains within this area would be disturbed, and probably totally destroyed.

Certain features in the fabric of the church indicated the possibility of a much earlier structure on or near the site. The most significant of these was the tower arch, which appears to be reset 12th-century work (**175**). Documentary references supported these observations: written sources indicate a church in 1550, and refer to a chapel of St James. In view of this evidence, there was clearly a need for major archaeological investigation in advance of the repairs. It was carried out by the Archaeology Unit of the former West Yorkshire Metropolitan County Council with the willing co-operation of the Reverend Alan Kitchen, the incumbent, and the church authorities; it was supported by the Ancient Monuments Inspectorate of the Department of the Environment. This chapter provides a summary of the main findings of the investigation, beginning with the earliest remains and ending with the 18th-century building. A fuller report of the discoveries is lodged with the excavation archive in the Sites and Monuments Record of the West Yorkshire Archaeology Service.

The account presented here is intended to show the amount of valuable information which may be buried behind (or within) the wallplaster and beneath the floors of even relatively unpromising churches; hence, it shows also what can be lost during structural repairs which are carried out without archaeological investigation.

The Excavations

The interior of the church was completely excavated by archaeological methods. The ground below the flooring had been extensively disturbed by burials (171), but the few relatively undisturbed patches were sufficient to demonstrate that two successive earlier structures had occupied the site of the 18th-century church. The remains of these buildings are described here, beginning with the first.

Building I

The earliest remains were very fragmentary wall foundations, discovered within the area of the present nave. They are illustrated on the first of the accompanying plans (169) which also indicates the extent of later intrusions, both structural and sepulchral. In the W half of the nave there were insubstantial footings of edge-set sandstone rubble pieces laid herringbone fashion, some incorporating water-worn pebbles. The footings appeared to represent a N wall (106; 138), a W (155), and a S wall (164). A related floor level of compact sandy material (134) was heavily burnt. Two post-holes (181; 182) were also possibly associated with this phase. The footings were narrow (only 0.3m wide), and so were possibly designed for a timber structure rather than full stone walls.

Further east, continuing roughly the same course and alignment, was a set of three more wall foundations of rather different character: they were formed of small, undressed sandstone pieces roughly laid in courses. N and S foundations (136; 130) had been so attenuated that their widths and even their precise alignments were uncertain; wall 136, for example, was cut away along its N side by the N side foundation trench of Building II. The N and S side foundations of Building I survived up to about 0.58m in width. A related N-S wall (137) linking the W ends of walls 130 and 136 had survived in patches, between graves, to its full width of about 1.3m. It is quite possible, though unproven, that the N and S walls had originally extended to a similar width. Patches of an associated sandy layer (183) probably again represented flooring. The surface of the layer was burnt, but not so heavily as 134 further west. It extended E slightly beyond the surviving E ends of the foundations 130 and 136.

These remains are interpreted as the earliest surviving ecclesiastical structures on this site. The difference in character between the footings in the E and W parts may indicate a building of two phases of construction – or at least two different kinds of superstructure. Their date of erection is unknown, since there were no datable finds associated with foundations or floor levels. The

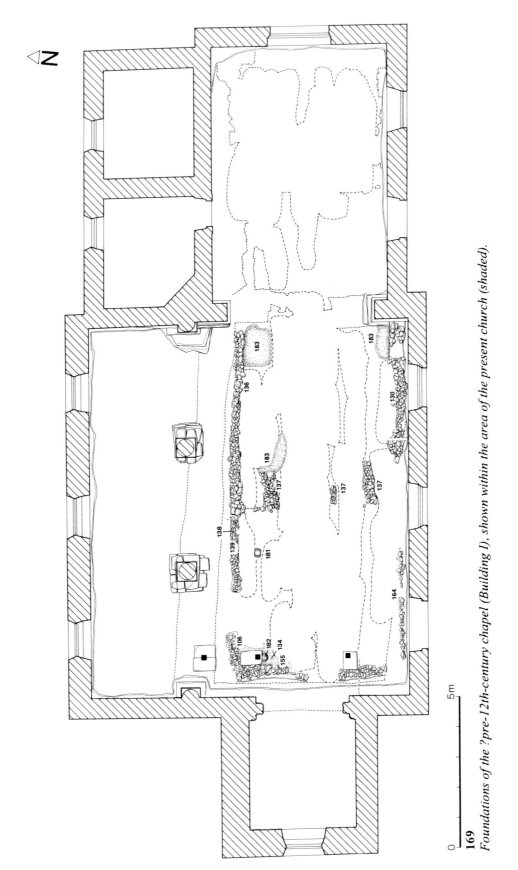

N

0   5m

169 *Foundations of the ?pre-12th-century chapel (Building I), shown within the area of the present church (shaded).*

121

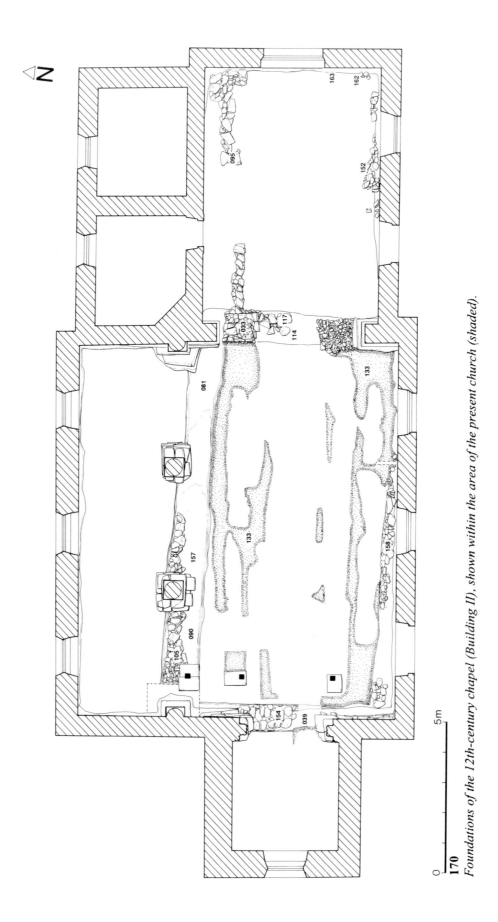

N

0 ___ 5m

170

Foundations of the 12th-century chapel (Building II), shown within the area of the present church (shaded).

122

replacement Building II was, however, constructed in the 12th century, on the evidence of architectural fragments presumed to have derived from it (see below). Unless there was a significant break in occupation, Building I would therefore have been in use during the 11th to 12th centuries; it may, of course, have been erected much earlier. There is no direct evidence that it was a church, but a grave-marker (**178**, No. 6) incorporated in the foundation of Building II indicates earlier ecclesiastical associations. Its E-W aligned, 'two-cell' plan is also suggestive of an early church.

Building II

The structure which replaced Building I was on a slightly different alignment; it was also slightly wider and possibly longer (**170**). Moreover, its plan form was more intelligible: a two-cell building comprising a nave and a stepped-in rectangular chancel. The wall foundations had largely been robbed out, and were marked mainly by trenches; but sufficient areas of stonework survived to indicate a foundation width of 1.1m. It was composed of roughly dressed sandstone rubble, mainly one course in height but surviving in places to two courses.

The nave N wall foundation ran beneath the aisle arcade of the 18th century. Part of its bottom course survived towards the W end (105) and incorporated a grave-marker (**178**, No. 6). The rest of the wall was signified by a robbed-out foundation trench (081; 090). The W and S nave walls (154; 158) were of similar construction to the N wall, and ran partly beneath the walls of the present church. Foundation 154 incorporated another sculptured stone (**178**, No. 7). The nave area thus defined contained the remnants of flooring (133), which overlay the flooring (134) of Building I. It consisted of a laminated layer of grey clay and sand with the surface compacted, burnished and worn. The laminates may have been the result of resurfacing; traces of vegetation between them may indicate a dressing of rushes or straw.

The wall dividing nave from chancel was marked by another robber trench (114) and an unrobbed stub of foundation (117) beneath the present chancel archway. The foundation supported a wall of neatly dressed blocks (033) chamfered on its S end; this presumably marked the N respond of the earlier chancel arch. Foundation 117 was bonded into the remnants of the N chancel foundation (095). The footings of the E and S chancel walls (162; 152) were situated more directly beneath the present walls.

The dating of Building II is provided by various architectural fragments recovered in the excavations. Two of these (**176**, Nos 1-2), decorated with chevron ornament, are assigned to the early 12th century; they presumably derived from a doorway. Other pieces are also Romanesque in style (**177**, Nos 3-4). More substantial evidence of a 12th-century date is provided by the present tower arch, discussed below.

The Present Building

Before investigations began there were a few indications of an earlier structure within the fabric of the present church. The external walls were almost all composed of closely jointed, squared sandstone blocks newly cut for the 18th-century building; but one wall, the N wall of the north aisle and vestry, appeared to be built of reused blocks. Internally the masonry could not be seen because plaster and wooden panelling entirely covered the walls; but the archway between the nave and tower could be identified as a reused 12th-century architectural feature (**173**), with scalloped capitals to the columns. It seems to have been elongated for use in the tower, and may

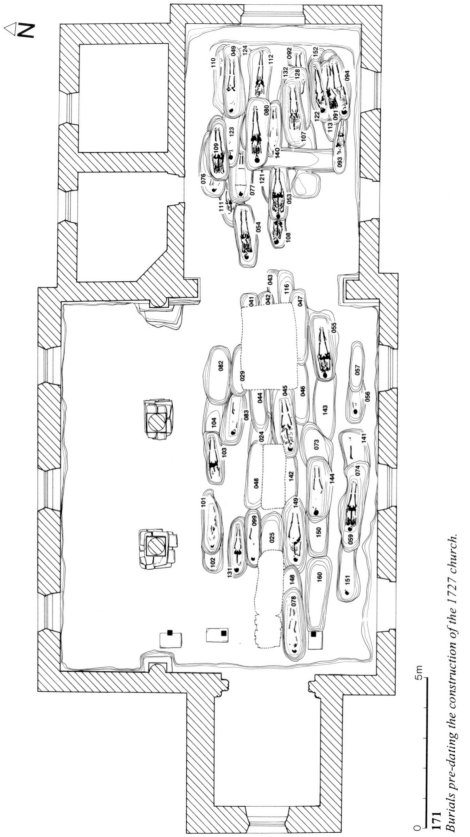

Burials pre-dating the construction of the 1727 church.

124

172

173

*The 18th-century fittings were reinstated (**172**) after the excavations (**173**).*

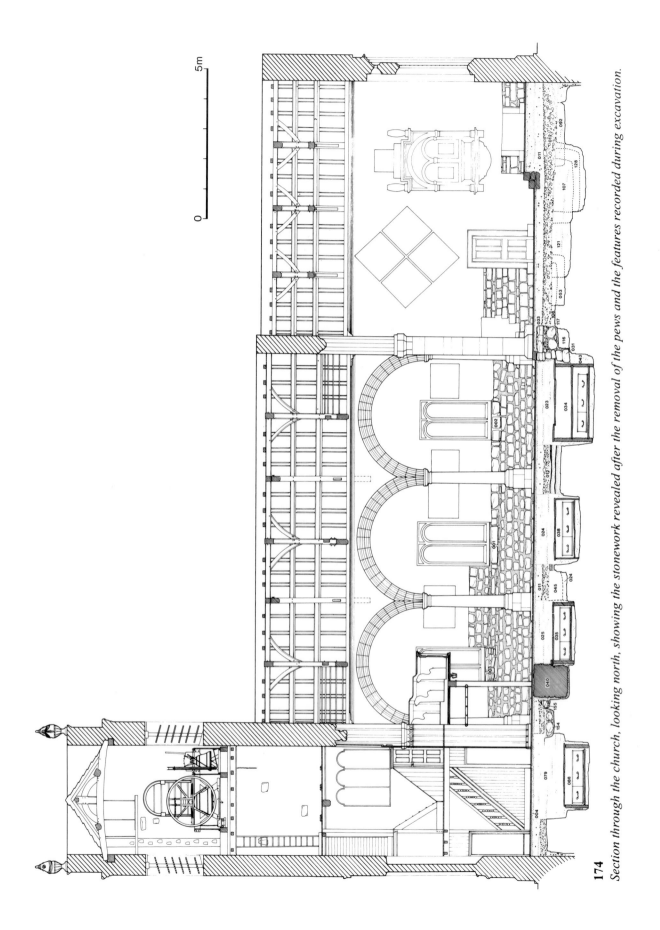

5m

174 *Section through the church, looking north, showing the stonework revealed after the removal of the pews and the features recorded during excavation.*

126

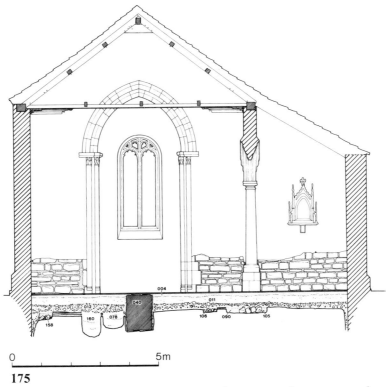

0   5m

175

Section through the west end of the nave, facing west, showing the tower arch, masonry and excavated features.

originally have been the chancel arch. Furthermore, the W window in the tower appears to contain medieval stonework in the Perpendicular style, indicating late medieval alterations to the earlier church; it was perhaps set originally in the E wall of the chancel, above the altar. The N aisle windows, largely restored and repositioned, probably date to the 15th or 16th century, and were presumably also rescued from the medieval building.

Only when the panelling had been removed from the internal wall face (**174**), however, did the scale of reuse become evident. It was marked in the first place by the tooling visible on the exposed surfaces of the stones: fine, narrow diagonal lines characteristic of Norman masonry. Secondly, many of the stones bore traces of painted plaster: some had fragments of black-letter texts, with indications of figurative work in several colours. The style of lettering would date the painting to the mid-16th century when, one might assume, a frieze of Biblical texts and illustrations had decorated the church. It was quite evident that the stones had been reused in new positions, as the paintwork indicated that some had been inverted, and others set at right-angles to their original orientations.

Further evidence of reuse, this time of timbers, was found beneath the pews. These had been seated on a solid framework of jointed oak joists; several of the beams forming joists had been used previously as roofing timbers.

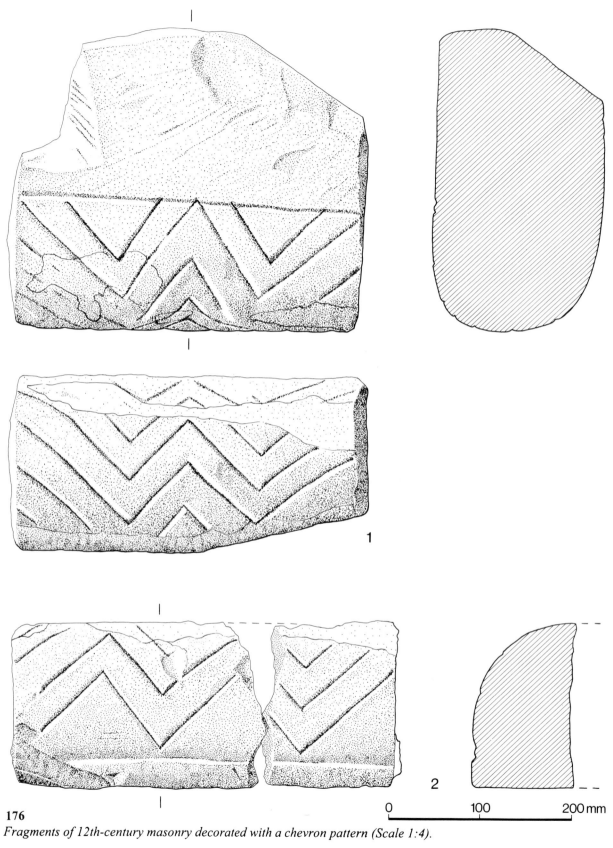

176

Fragments of 12th-century masonry decorated with a chevron pattern (Scale 1:4).

1

2

0   100   200 mm

128

Sculptured Stones

by Peter Ryder

Architectural Fragments

A small number of Romanesque architectural fragments were recovered during the excavations in the church (**176, 177**):

1 & 2   Two fragments which appear from their D-shaped section to have been pieces of either the jamb of a doorway or the respond of an arch. They bear a chevron pattern which extends right round the curved section of the jamb; the lines of the pattern are quite lightly incised, with little attempt at relief modelling, and the pattern is bounded by a single incised border on each face. This rather primitive form of a popular Romanesque ornament suggests a date near the beginning of the 12th century; its affinities are more with the simple geometric patterns found on some sepulchral monuments of the late 11th and early 12th centuries than with the more conventional chevron seen on the later Romanesque arch voussoirs. In addition, the use of the ornament on the vertical jamb of a doorway is much less common. At Adel, chevron in its fully developed and more deeply carved form is used in this way in the third order of the sumptuous south doorway of *c.* 1160, but the section of the Tong fragments suggests they formed the jambs of the inner or possibly sole order of an opening. S*F 1397: context 180 (E of present church); SF 1399: unstratified*

3   An elongate stone bearing two relief-carved masks; their spacing suggests that they were part of a longer series. The long axis of the stone has a slight curve, suggesting that it may have formed part of one order (or a hoodmould) of a large arch, rather than a section of an ornamental string-course. The masks are simply carved, and framed by what appears to be some simple form of head-dress, perhaps implying that they are intended to represent females. The use of repetitive series of masks is often seen in Romanesque churches (e.g. the external corbel table at Adel). *SF1398: context 026 (base for the present chancel steps)*

4   A stone that might be part of the same decorative scheme as No. 3 above, but its details have been erased by damage and weathering. *SF unrecorded: unstratified*

5   Not illustrated. A narrow slab with a three-quarter roll moulding at one angle. There is not enough detail to ascribe to it even an approximate date. The most noteworthy feature is the stone type, which is a coarse gritstone, unlike the other architectural fragments which are all a fawn sandstone. *SF 1226: context 165 (material from foundation 117, marking nave/chancel wall of Building II)*

Stones with incised patterns

In addition to the architectural fragments a large number of stones (totalling over 50, although many are small fragments) bear what appear to be incised patterns; all of these were found reused in the 11th and 12th-century foundations (**178**):

6   A stone which appears from its form to be a grave-marker. Roughly shaped slab bearing, on both faces, patterns made up of incised lines often terminating in broader indents.

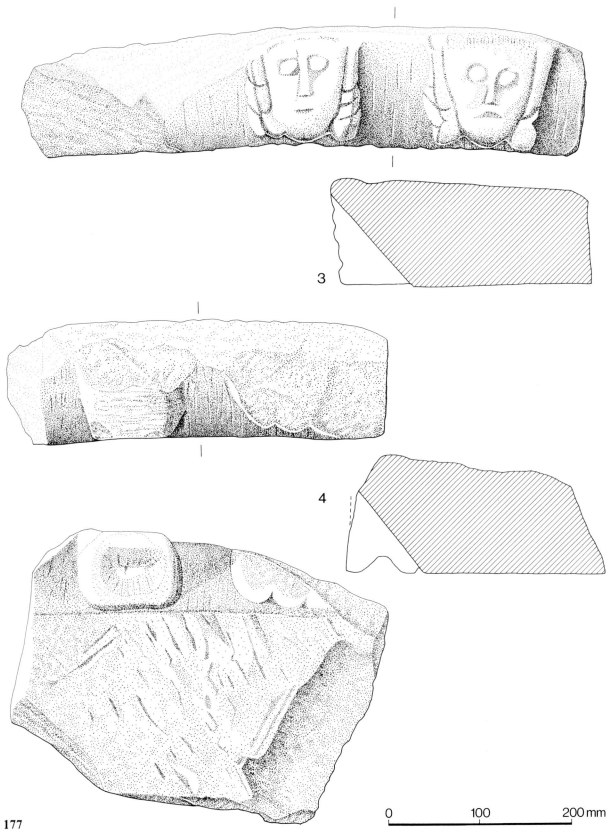

177
Fragments of ?12th-century masonry, possibly from a large arch, decorated with relief-carved masks (Scale 1:4).

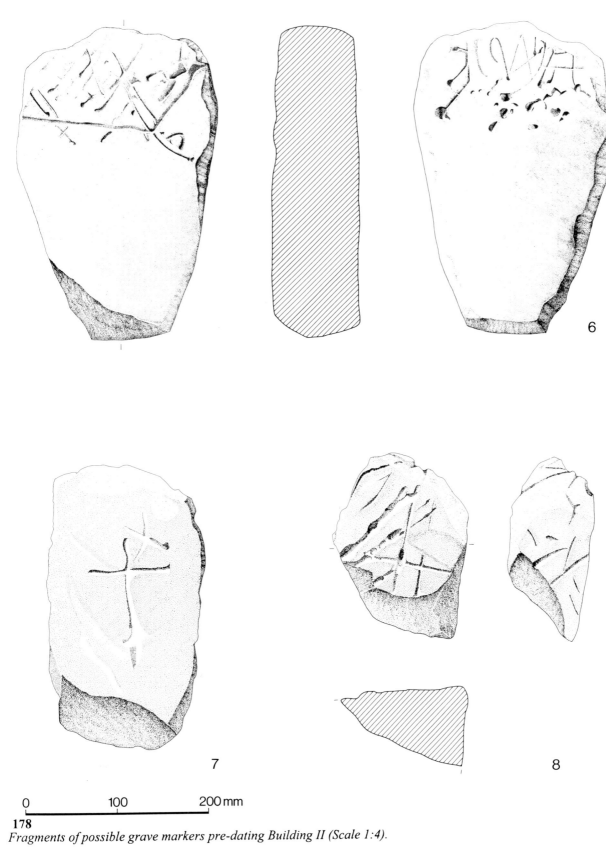

6

7

8

178

Fragments of possible grave markers pre-dating Building II (Scale 1:4).

The tapering lower section of the stone has been left blank, presumably for insertion into the ground. On neither side do the patterns of criss-crossing lines and indents make up any recognisable or even remotely geometric motifs. The early headstones from Adel (now in Leeds City Museum), found reused in the footings of the mid-12th-century church there, might be cited as rough parallels, although even the crudest of these shows lines and indents making up patterns with some rough symmetry about them. The Adel stones are usually ascribed to the 11th century but lack stylistic parallels in the area. *SF 1396: context 105 (part of N nave foundation of Building II)*

7   An unshaped piece of sandstone which includes what may be an intentional cross at the centre of its main face. *SF 1252: context 154 (part of W wall foundation of Building II)*

8   One of numerous pieces which appear to be unshaped lumps of sandstone, ranging from fragments with a single scratch or incised line, to some larger pieces with what appear to be more elaborate but incomprehensible scratchings and dots. *SF 1315: context 164 (S wall footing of Building I, W end).*

It is difficult to make any useful comment on this material. The evidence of the two or possibly three slabs which seem from their form to be headstones suggests that the others may be pieces of similar monuments. It is difficult to understand why any carver should incise apparently random patterns on such crude and unworked lumps of sandstone; the imaginative mind might see an illiterate attempt to simulate runic lettering in the parallel lines on some of the stones. Carving that has degenerated into mere incised doodlings, and half-remembered runes would both be possible in the early 11th century, but are far removed from the county's tradition of good-quality pre-Conquest sculpture exemplified at several sites quite close to Tong, such as Bradford, and more notably Dewsbury; most of the Tong fragments might equally well be prehistoric scratchings rather than Christian grave markers.

Gazetteer

of

Medieval Churches

and Chapels

Parish church

+ Chapel

Modern county boundary

Modern county boundary which does not coincide with ancient parish boundary

Ancient parish boundary

Extra-parochial area

0   10   20 km

179

Map showing medieval churches and chapels included in the gazetteer.

134

Gazetteer of Medieval Churches and Chapels

This gazetteer covers all the churches and chapels included in the churches survey. Each of these has been the subject of a level 2 investigation, similar to the Featherstone example set out in Chapter Eleven; copies of these reports are lodged in the West Yorkshire Sites and Monuments Record, held by the Archaeology Service at 14 St John's North, Wakefield WF1 3QA. In the following gazetteer, an illustration of each church is accompanied by a short account, which is merely a brief precis of the major points covered in the full report. Numbers in bold refer to illustrations elsewhere in this volume.

ABERFORD
St Ricarius

The only ancient part of Aberford church is the 12th-century west tower; as at Bramham and Ledsham, which have very similar towers, the embattled parapet is a late medieval addition. The octagonal spire is probably late medieval work as well, although it may have been rebuilt in the early 19th century. The body of the church is of 1861, replacing a smaller late 11th or early 12th-century building which had much herringbone work. A small 12th-century window and a 13th-century lancet have been reset in the sanctuary walls. Three Anglo-Saxon cross fragments are preserved in the church; propped against the west wall of the churchyard is a medieval stone coffin. *See also* **33, 148, 149, 150**.

ACKWORTH
St Cuthbert

The body of the church was rebuilt after an 1852 fire, leaving only the old west tower which is of the usual 15th-century type. Inside the church the battered bowl of a plain early Norman font rests on what looks like the base of a 14th-century quatrefoil-section pier; there is a second font dated 1663 with an interesting inscription. Mounted on the north aisle wall is a fine cross slab floorstone to Robert Hopton (d. 1506), and in the churchyard close to the tower is an earlier cross slab of an unusual type (see also Darrington, Kippax and Methley) designed to be laid in a churchyard rather than inside the church. An important armorial slab to Thomas Bradley (d. 1673; he was Rector of Ackworth and chaplain to Charles I) is mounted on the vestry wall; it has recently been restored.

ADDINGHAM
St Peter

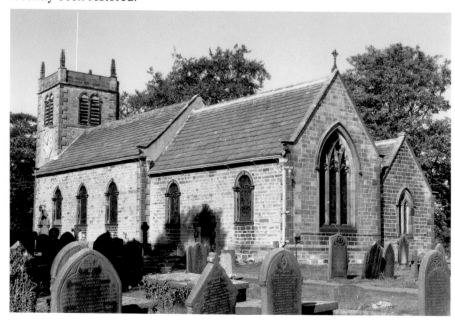

St Peter's consists of a nave with a three-bay north aisle, a west tower, and a chancel with a north chapel and vestry. Set away from the village in an Iron Age ditched enclosure high above the Wharfe, this church stands on what is potentially one of the most exciting archaeological sites in West Yorkshire. At first sight the church is an attractive little Georgian building (the tower has a '1757' inscription), but this is just the result of the recasing of an older structure. The nave retains a fine late medieval roof, and the north arcade and aisle are 15th-century work; the north wall of the nave is older still, and could conceivably be pre-Conquest. The west gallery and font date from the 18th-century alterations. An Anglo-Saxon cross shaft is on display; other fragments of early sculpture were found recently when the interior of the tower was replastered, but have been covered over again. *See also* p. 22; **29, 100, 136, 137.**

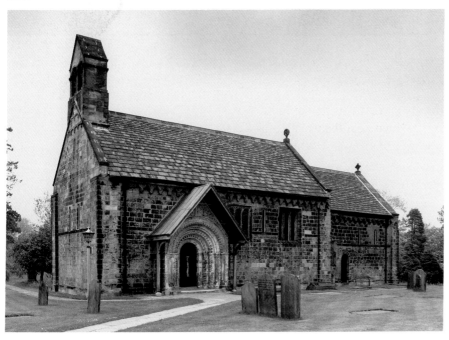

ADEL
St John the Baptist

By far the finest Norman church in the county, it consists only of a nave and chancel, with a Victorian north vestry. Although simple in plan it is quite spacious; the most sumptuous features are the south door (which has a spectacular closing ring of *c.* 1200) and the chancel arch. The gable over the door has carvings of Christ in Majesty and the emblems of the Four Evangelists; some of the symbolism on the chancel arch still defies interpretation. The Victorians returned the church to something closer to its original state; the present bell-cote is of 1839 and several of the windows of 1879. The 15th-century east window, now reset in the 1879 vestry, has some good early 18th-century painted glass. Beside the churchyard gate a collection of worked stones includes a coffin and a capital which may be Roman; in Leeds City Museum are four very strange headstones, found last century, incorporated in the foundations of the present church; they may be Anglo-Saxon or early Norman work, but there is nothing else like them in the county. *See also* pp 29-30; **37-41, 47, 153.**

ALMONDBURY
All Hallows

A large and interesting church consisting of a five-bay aisled nave with west tower and south porch, and a chancel with side chapels. The side walls of the nave above the arcades are of uncertain date; they are presumably older than the eastern extension of the chancel which has two late 13th-century windows. Everything else looks to date from a late 15th to early 16th-century remodelling, except for the eastern bays of the chancel chapels and the embattled parapets with their pinnacles, which are late 19th century; the drawing above shows the church before these additions. The nave ceiling, with gilded bosses and a long inscription dated 1522, is probably the finest in the county. Fifteenth-century glass with figures of saints is preserved in two of the windows of the north chapel; a section of the medieval rood beam is kept in the same chapel. The font has a fine 16th-century canopy. *See also* p. 67; **66, 104, 105, 151**.

BADSWORTH
St Mary the Virgin

Badsworth church has a nave with three-bay aisles extending to embrace the west tower, a Victorian south porch, and a chancel with a two-bay north aisle and a 19th-century north-east vestry. The nave walls may be Norman (see architectural fragments displayed in the south aisle), and the chancel arcade and the reset nave north door are of the 13th century. The rest of the church was remodelled around 1400, in a style transitional between Decorated and Perpendicular. There are some interesting monuments: a 14th-century cross slab in the chancel floor, a large monument to Sir John Bright (1688), and various tombs in the churchyard including one to Osmond Alexander (d. 1788), 'a native of Asia from the capital of Hindostan'. *See also* pp 64-65; **102**.

BARDSEY
All Hallows

This well-known church consists of a nave with three-bay aisles extended west to embrace the tower, a south porch, and a chancel with a north chapel and a south vestry. The nave walls and tower (which may have been raised on an earlier porch, as at Ledsham) are Anglo-Saxon. The north aisle was added *c.* 1125 and the south aisle late in the 12th century; both aisles may incorporate masonry of Anglo-Saxon *porticus* at their west ends. In the early 14th century the chancel was rebuilt, and the nave aisles widened later in the same century. The north chapel is probably of late medieval date; the vestry was added in 1724 as a Bayley family chapel. The church, and in particular its Anglo-Saxon phases, still poses many problems; it is worth taking a long look at the west elevation as an example of 'above-ground archaeology'. There is a fine Norman south door, reset in the 14th century, and a variety of carved stones and monuments inside the church. *See also* pp 16, 37; **5, 6, 21, 22, 44, 48, 57, 153**.

BARWICK IN ELMET
All Saints

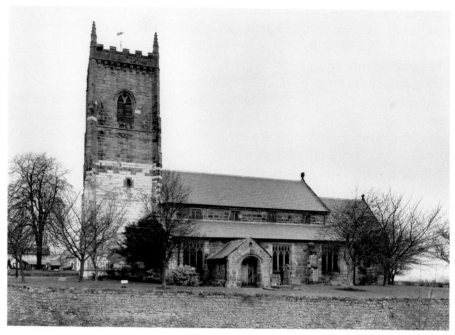

All Saints has a four-bay aisled nave with a west tower, south porch, and a chancel with a north vestry. The nave and chancel walls may be late 11th or early 12th century, with herringbone masonry (as at Kippax). The chancel was remodelled early in the 14th century, and the nave aisles added around 1400. The tower has a worn inscription dated 1455, asking prayers for the soul of Henry Vavasour. There are two Anglo-Saxon carved stones in the south aisle; set against the north aisle wall is a cross slab floorstone to John Gascoigne (d. 1445). The similarities with Kippax, both in masonry and in original ground plan, are interesting: Barwick replaced Kippax as the administrative centre for this part of the Honour of Pontefract around 1100. Both villages have early earthwork castles. *See also* p. 27; **35**, **95**.

BATLEY
All Saints

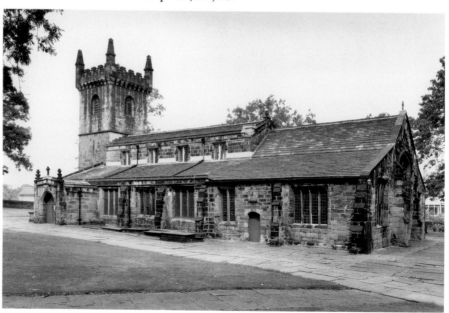

This church consists of a three-bay aisled nave with a west tower and south porch, and a two-bay chancel with flanking chapels and a modern north vestry. The nave walls and lower part of the tower are probably 12th century, and the south arcade (with quatrefoil piers) and chancel arch are of the 1300s; the rest of the church was remodelled in the half century either side of 1500. Unlike many it escaped the Victorian era relatively lightly; most of the windows still have their 16th or 17th-century plain square-headed or round-arched lights. Note the rood stair at the east end of the south arcade, the late 15th-century screen in the north chapel, the late 16th-century (Renaissance) screen in the south chapel, and, outside, medieval cross slabs built into the west end of the south aisle and nave clerestory. The broad churchyard is now a municipal park, with decaying 18th and 19th-century grave slabs used to pave paths. *See also* **152**.

**BEESTON
St Mary**

The medieval chapel of Beeston, shown in the old drawing above, seems to have consisted of an aisleless nave (?12th century) with a chancel (?13th century) that had a late 15th-century south chapel. A 1789 faculty details the remodelling of the building into what we would now call a 'preaching box', retaining some of the original external walls but enlarging the nave to the south. In 1877 the present chancel was built onto the end of the old chapel, the remainder of which was demolished and replaced by the present nave and aisles in 1885-86. The east window of the old south chapel was reset in the corresponding position in the 19th-century church (along with its remains of early 16th-century glass); various 12th-century architectural fragments found in the old walls were reconstructed as an archway in the vestry wall, now partly hidden by furniture. There is a mid-17th-century font.

BINGLEY
All Saints

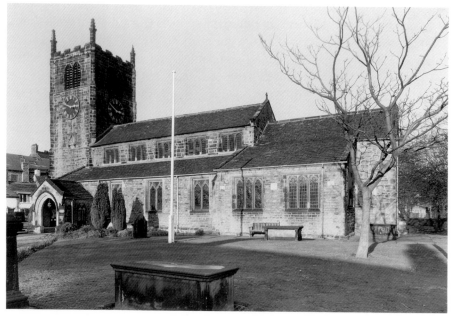

Bingley parish church has a four-bay aisled nave with a west tower, south porch and modern north vestries, and a two-bay aisled chancel. There may be 13th-century masonry in the chancel, but most of the old features of the church date from the usual late 15th and early 16th-century changes; the chancel is said to have been remodelled in 1518 by Richard Wylson, Prior of Drax. The church was altered again in the 18th century: the tower was heightened in 1739 and the south aisle and chancel chapels Classicised before being returned to the Gothic by the inevitable Victorian restoration (1871). The nave has a fine king-post roof. There is an ancient font with a lengthy inscription in runes that has perplexed antiquaries, and a fragment of an Anglo-Saxon cross shaft.

BIRSTALL
St Peter

Birstall church was completely rebuilt in 1863-70 except for the west tower; the lower part of this is 12th century and the belfry 15th century. The old church was a sprawling late medieval structure typical of the area; its successor is larger, but retains the same overall appearance. Inside there is a 'museum corner' in each aisle, and quite a number of items of interest: a late Anglo-Saxon cross base with a tree-like design, several medieval grave slabs and carved bench ends, and a 12th-century font bowl.

BRADFORD
The Cathedral
Church of St Peter

The medieval parts of Bradford Cathedral consist of a nine-bay aisled nave with a west tower, and sections of the two-bay chapels that flanked the old chancel. The latter was replaced by the present central tower and eastern arm in 1958-63. The nave walls are of 12th or 13th-century date; the arcades may be of 14th-century date but have various puzzling features suggesting that they may have been reused. The aisles are said to have been built (or rebuilt?) in the early 1400s and a remodelling of the church was completed in 1458. The nave clerestory was added in 1493 and then the massive west tower, the best feature of the cathedral, was built in 1493-1508; it is clear both internally and externally that the tower was built as a free-standing structure, and then joined to the church by a westward extension of the nave. There are two pieces of Anglo-Saxon cross shaft, one built into the north aisle wall and one by the door to the new St Aidan's Chapel. The font is Victorian, but the font cover is an impressive piece of early 16th-century work. *See also* pp 74, 100; **117**.

BRAMHAM
All Saints

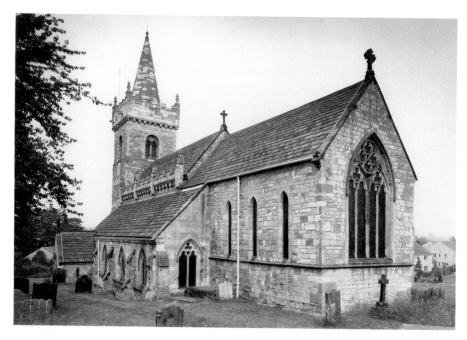

A church consisting of a three-bay aisled nave with a west tower and a Victorian south porch, and a chancel with 19th-century side chapels. Despite a heavy 'restoration' in 1853 the structural development of the church can be interpreted as follows: an Anglo-Saxon nave, with north aisle and tower (like those at Aberford and Ledsham) added in the mid-12th century; south aisle (with a good south door) added and chancel rebuilt in the 13th century, and the embattled parapets of nave and tower added in the late 15th century. Inside there is an interesting 12th-century headstone and a little late medieval woodwork; but the most impressive thing at Bramham is the churchyard, a great oval raised above the surrounding roads. Does this mark a pre-Conquest monastic enclosure? The position of the church at one end hints that there may have been another early church in the centre. See also pp 17, 33; **23, 42, 46**.

CALVERLEY
St Wilfrid

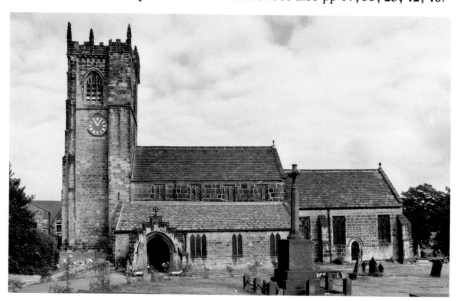

Calverley parish church consists of a four-bay aisled nave with a west tower and south porch, and a chancel with a two-bay north chapel and a north vestry. The nave walls are of 11th or early 12th-century date, but only one architectural feature has survived from that period: a blocked window above the south arcade which has its external, round-arched head cut from a single block of stone. It is impossible to say whether the window is pre-Conquest or later. The tower is 13th or early 14th century, altered later in the 14th century when the chancel was rebuilt; the nave aisles and top stage of the tower were added in the 15th century. The nave aisles and chancel were rebuilt in 1869, although the latter is more or less a copy of its medieval predecessor. There is a good collection of medieval cross slabs under the tower, as well as one Anglo-Saxon fragment, and medieval glass in the east window. The font has a good Jacobean cover. *See also* p. 50; **81, 82**.

CASTLEFORD
All Saints

The medieval parish church here was, like its successor, a cruciform building with an aisled nave. The basic structure might have been 12th century (one report mentions a 'Norman' arch) but the chancel would seem to have been rebuilt around 1300, and the whole church remodelled (with the addition of the south aisle) in the 15th century. The nave received a north aisle in 1853, which was retained when the rest of the building was rebuilt in 1866. The photograph above was taken sometime between these two dates. The most interesting aspect of the site is its Roman origins: Roman pottery is still being picked up in the churchyard, and the building seems to have been located within the area of Castleford's late Roman defences, by the side of the main north to south road. Inside the church is a restored section of medieval screen, but this is an 'import' from Methley; the only real relic of the old All Saints is its much-scraped font, probably 12th century, now in the 20th-century church at Glasshoughton. *See also* pp 9-10; **13, 14**.

CLECKHEATON
White Chapel

The present building is a 'preaching box' chapel erected in 1820-21 on the site of an older building, which is shown in the drawing above. Several relics of the old chapel survive. There is a fine carved font of *c.* 1100 with motifs including a *sheila-na-gig* (a Celtic fertility figure). In the porch is a 12th-century cross slab. Various carved stones, including a door lintel of 1706 from the predecessor of the present chapel, have been reset in the fabric. In the crowded graveyard are an ancient yew tree and an early 18th-century font. *See also* p. 36; **56**.

COLLINGHAM
St Oswald

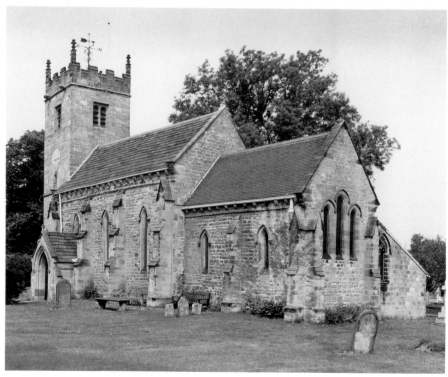

A small church with a nave having a three-bay north aisle, west tower and south porch, and a chancel with an 1898 north vestry. The core of an Anglo-Saxon church consisting of nave and a small box-like chancel survives; the north aisle may have been added around 1200 and widened in the 14th century, the chancel extended in the 13th century, and the tower built in the 16th century. A heavy-handed 'restoration' of 1840-41, with applied plaster mouldings to the arcade arches, nave roof trusses and a simulated vault beneath the tower, is just about distant enough in time to take on an interest in itself. There are two Anglo-Saxon cross shafts (which may indicate a pre-Viking monastery site) and a few medieval and post-medieval monuments of interest. *See also* pp 16-17, 93; **143**.

CROFTON
All Saints

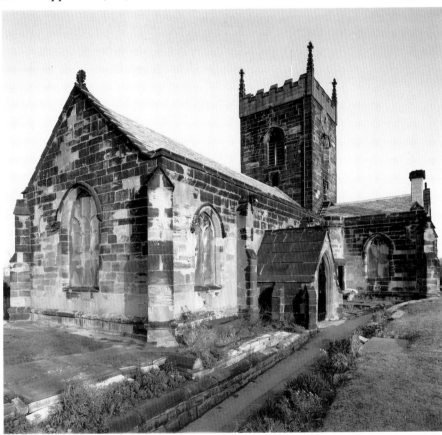

Crofton church on its hilltop site is an aisleless cruciform building with a central tower and a south porch. The whole structure, in a fairly plain Perpendicular style, seems to have been built *c*. 1430 by Richard Fleming, Bishop of Lincoln, as a gift to his native village. There was an earlier church (there are two Anglo-Saxon cross fragments in the north transept), but this seems to have been on a different site, now lost. Several interesting grave slabs, including one commemorating a 16th-century vicar, were recently uncovered when the chancel was reordered, and have been reset in the new floor. Outside is a medieval coffin and a 1922 lychgate made out of the timbers of the 17th-century bell frames. *See also* p. 70; **92, 110, 111, 155**.

DARRINGTON
St Luke and All Saints

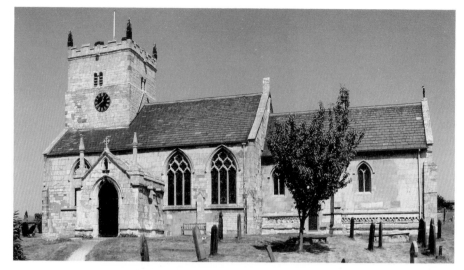

A church which consists of a three-bay nave with aisles extending to embrace the west tower, a south porch, and a chancel with a north chapel. It is not a building that one can do justice to in a short paragraph! The visitor with an antiquarian bent will want to spend quite some time here. A conjectural outline of the building history might be: Anglo-Saxon church with a west tower, the tower being remodelled with a new belfry in the later 12th century; aisles added and chancel rebuilt in the early 13th century; aisles heightened and porch and the interesting chancel chapel added in the 14th century; chancel remodelled in the 15th century (when the west side of the tower seems to have fallen down and been rebuilt as well), with further alterations and new roofs around 1500. The evidence for post-medieval changes was largely removed by Sir Arthur Blomfield's attentions in 1880. The monuments include two good effigies and another of the unusual cross slabs (compare Ackworth and Kippax) designed to lie outside in the churchyard; there are several late medieval seats and bench ends. *See also* pp 20, 22, 49-50; **28, 80**.

DEWSBURY
All Saints

148

All Saints now consists of a four-bay aisled nave with a west tower, and a late 19th-century eastern arm with crossing, transepts and aisled chancel; the drawing shows the pre-Victorian church. Only the ghost of the Anglo-Saxon minster survives in a ragged band of masonry and the remnants of angle quoins above the 13th-century nave arcades; Anglo-Saxon evidence is more easily appreciated in the fine display of carved stones at the west end of the north aisle. The wheel cross, with an inscription commemorating Paulinus' preaching here in AD 627, is a palpable early 19th-century fake. The Anglo-Saxon nave was extended to the east before the addition of aisles in the 13th century; all signs of later medieval alterations (except for the panelled nave ceiling with its gilded bosses) have been swept away by 18th and 19th-century rebuilding. The north aisle and west tower are rather attractive pseudo-Gothic of 1765-67, designed by John Carr; thankfully they escaped the late 19th-century rebuilding of the south aisle and eastern parts. The north arcade, and in particular its clustered piers, is a striking piece of mid-13th-century architecture. As well as the Anglo-Saxon stones there is a good collection of medieval cross slabs and post-medieval monuments, a 17th-century font, and some excellent 14th and 15th-century glass in the north transept. *See also* pp 17-18, 40-42, 88-89; **15, 17, 24, 25, 64, 132, 138, 139**.

**EAST ARDSLEY
St Michael**

The medieval church at East Ardsley was demolished in 1881; ten years earlier Sir Stephen Glynne described it as consisting of a nave with a later four-bay north aisle 'in debased style', a small 'modern' west tower, a 'rickety' south porch, and a chancel with a north vestry. This is the building shown in the drawing above. The south door, inside the porch, was reset as the entrance to the new church which was built a little to the north of the site of its predecessor; it is a good early 12th-century piece with saltire crosses and beakheads. A three-light Perpendicular window with unusual carvings of flowers and a cat-like head on the inner frame was also saved and stands in the vicarage garden. The present church also preserves a '1663' font. *See also* **49**.

ELLAND
St Mary the Virgin

Elland parish church, in the medieval period a chapel within the parish of Halifax, consists of a four-bay nave with aisles extending to engage the west tower, a south porch, and a chancel with two-bay side chapels. The chancel arch is of *c.* 1175, later reconstructed to a pointed form, and the nave has the earliest church roof (?13th century) in the county. The nave aisles and chancel chapels have 14th-century style windows, although these may have been reset in a late 15th-century remodelling, when the east window (which retains its glass, dated to *c.* 1490) was inserted and the church was left much in its present form; although there were extensive 17th and 18th-century alterations erased as usual by the Victorians. Beneath the chancel is a crypt or bone hole, much altered but retaining its original stair cut into the thickness of the south wall and descending from the side of the altar. There are two pairs of medieval stalls, a '1662' font, and a variety of post-medieval wall monuments. *See also* pp 34, 46; **74, 135**.

EMLEY
St Michael

150

Emley is a typical 'Pennine' church, consisting of a three-bay nave with a north aisle, south porch and a rather massive west tower; the chancel has a two-bay north aisle, with a small vestry north of the aisle. The building history is especially hard to disentangle (matters are complicated by a local tradition, backed up by some place-name evidence, that the early medieval church stood on a different site). The north wall of the nave and its north-east quoins appear 12th century in character, and there are many 12th-century architectural fragments reused in the present fabric, including a tympanum with two beasts (a lamb and a lion?) above a piscina on the south wall of the nave. The nave may have been partly rebuilt (possibly incorporating an older south aisle) in the 13th or 14th century, then the whole church was remodelled in the late 15th or early 16th century, with the addition of tower, north aisle and chancel chapel. The chapel was extended to form a burial chapel for the Assheton family in 1632. Apart from the reused architectural fragments there are a number of cross slabs incorporated in the fabric; nave and porch roofs are probably of late medieval date, and show some unusual features. Two of the chancel windows retain 15th-century glass. *See also* **52, 98**.

**FEATHERSTONE
All Saints**

This church has a three-bay nave with a south aisle, west tower and south porch, and a three-bay chancel with a south chapel. The nave is probably of 12th-century date, and may have had a south aisle added in the 13th century; there was a general remodelling around 1400 and further alterations in the late 15th century, when the east end of the chancel and chapel was rebuilt and the present panelled chancel ceiling constructed. Most of the windows are of plain 16th and 17th-century type; there was a major but quite conservative restoration in 1878. The church has a good carved 15th-century font said to have been brought from Pontefract, and there is a full ring of three medieval bells. *See also* Chapter Eleven.

FELKIRK
St Peter

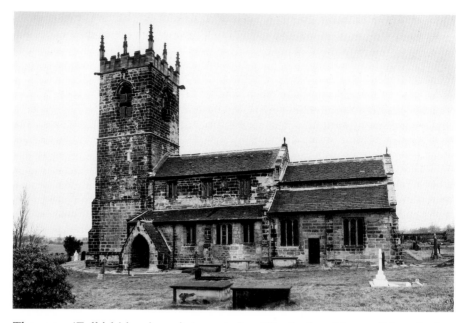

The name 'Felkirk' has been interpreted as 'Plank church', possibly referring to a pre-Conquest timber building. The present stone church has a three-bay aisled nave with a west tower and south porch, and a two-bay chancel with flanking chapels and a north-east sacristy. The earliest visible phase of the building is seen in the walling at the angles of the nave, with herringbone masonry visible at the south-east angle. The present 15th-century tower arch incorporates the reset jambs and capitals of a fine arch of *c.* 1100, probably part of this first build, and there are many other reused architectural fragments. The later medieval work is rather plainer: the south aisle is a 13th-century addition; the interesting little vaulted sacristy and the south porch are late 14th or early 15th century, and everything else is the product of a remodelling around 1500. The north arcade and tower arch may have been heightened in the 17th or 18th century to facilitate the insertion of galleries; many of the windows seem to be of this period as well. *See also* p. 27; **34, 36**.

FERRYBRIDGE
St Andrew

It is debatable whether one can class the present St Andrew's church in Ferrybridge as a medieval building, as it is neither in its original form nor on its original site. The church formerly stood at Ferry Fryston, between the main east coast railway line and the modern power station, on a site prone to flooding. The medieval building, shown here, consisted of a nave with a two-bay north aisle, a small west tower built within the body of the nave, a south porch, and a chancel with a two-bay north chapel. The nave was of late 12th-century date, with a cross-wall and arch carrying a western bell-cote or belfry added soon after; the chancel was rebuilt in the late 13th or 14th century. In the 15th century the north aisle and north chapel were added, and the older belfry converted into a small masonry tower. The south porch was probably of 18th or early 19th-century date, and there was a restoration with some regothicisation of windows, etc., in 1878. In 1952-53 the church was dismantled and moved to Ferrybridge; it was rebuilt utilising old stone and all its major architectural features, but in its reconstituted form the aisle and chapel have been put on the south rather than the north side, and the nave has been lengthened by one bay. *See also* pp 37-38, 70-71.

GARFORTH
St Mary

The medieval church at Garforth, shown here before demolition in 1844, was a fairly small building consisting of a nave with a west tower, perhaps a north aisle, a south porch and an aisleless chancel. It was probably largely of 15th-century date; the foundations of an older building 'in the Early English style' were seen when it was pulled down. A few architectural fragments and two medieval cross slabs lie in the churchyard; other material (along with some from the old church at Aberford) was taken by the Gascoigne family to build a folly in Parlington Park 2km to the north. This is itself now a sad and overgrown ruin; one mossy fragment of 15th-century tracery may have come from the east window of the old church at Garforth.

GUISELEY
St Oswald

The old parts of Guiseley church (extended to the north in 1910) consist of a nave with a three-bay south aisle, a west tower, a south porch, and a chancel with a south chapel. Despite a lot of Victorian and early 20th-century alteration this is still a most interesting building. It is not clear whether the nave walls are of Anglo-Saxon or very early Norman date: the south-east angle quoin looks Anglo-Saxon in character, and the remains of a small window obviously pre-date the rather fine mid-12th-century south arcade. The chancel seems to have been rebuilt in the later 12th century, and had two transept-like chapels added in the mid-13th century. The north aisle, west tower, and former south porch date to the 15th century. There was a major 'restoration' in 1866 when the south aisle and porch were rebuilt. The Norman south door, contemporary with the arcade, survives intact. The arches from the chancel to the transeptal chapels show detached shafts, very like the piers of the north arcade at Dewsbury; the south window of the surviving south chapel shows the beginnings of plate tracery, and is unique in the county. There is an Anglo-Saxon cross shaft in the base of the tower. *See also* pp 20, 41-42, 45; **45, 50, 65, 67, 99, 154**.

HALIFAX
St John the Baptist

Halifax is without a doubt the largest and most impressive of the late medieval churches in the county. The five-bay aisled nave has a west tower, a south porch, and a three-bay outer south aisle (the Holdsworth Chapel); the five-bay chancel has full-length chapels and an outer two-bay north aisle (the Rokeby Chapel). The structural development of the building has never been properly interpreted; it would seem that a sizable early medieval church, which was probably cruciform, was remodelled over a number of building campaigns during the 15th century. The only pre-15th-century features visible are the north wall of the north aisle which has three 14th-century windows, and a large number of reused 12th-century architectural fragments and carved stones scattered all round the building. The complexities of the building are exemplified by the chancel arch piers with their three levels of capitals, and the remains of two sets of rood stairs in the chancel south chapel. The Rokeby and Holdsworth Chapels date to 1533 and ?1554 respectively. Sir George Gilbert Scott and his son J.O. Scott carried out a major restoration in 1879. The monuments include several medieval cross slabs and many post-medieval wall tablets. The fittings and furnishings include much of great interest: the font is of 15th-century date, with an impressive contemporary canopy; there are late medieval stalls in the chancel and screens to the chapels, early 17th-century pews throughout the nave and aisles, and fine altar rails of 1698. *See also* pp 75, 77; **89, 119-23, 155.**

HAREWOOD
All Saints

The old parish church of Harewood now stands alone in the park of Harewood House near the site of the medieval village; the nave has four-bay aisles extended west to engage the tower, a south porch, and a chancel with flanking chapels and a 19th-century north vestry. The entire building is of early 15th-century date, apart from some relatively minor late 18th and 19th-century alterations; there are a few hints that older fabric is incorporated. Recent excavations have uncovered 12th and 14th-century architectural fragments. The collection of late medieval alabaster monuments is the glory of Harewood church; there are six pairs of effigies dating from *c.* 1419 to *c.* 1510. The church is now in the care of the Redundant Churches Fund and is (at the time of writing) open only on Wednesday and Sunday afternoons between May and October. *See also* pp 69-70; **107, 108, 109, 155.**

HARTSHEAD
St Peter

St Peter's has a three-bay aisled nave with a west tower and a south porch, and a chancel with a north vestry and organ chamber. The medieval church here had been altered more heavily than most in the 17th and 18th centuries: the arcade piers had been replaced in wood, and the consequent restoration in 1881 was more in the nature of a rebuilding. The oldest parts of the present building are the mid-12th-century chancel arch and south door, but apart from these, the very plain late medieval (or ?post-medieval) tower, the nave roof timbers (?17th century) and some walling in the north aisle and chancel, the whole building is Victorian. There is some attractive 17th and 18th-century woodwork in the church; the churchyard has quite a number of interesting memorials and a '1611' sundial. *See also* **54, 55**.

HAWORTH
St Michael and
All Angels

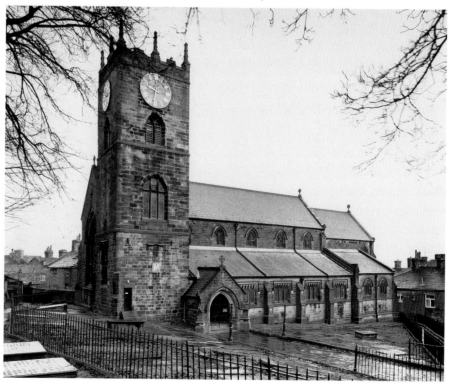

For most people the main interest of this church lies in its Brontë associations; the entire structure is of 1897 except for the tower (now at the west end of the south aisle) which was retained from the earlier church. This building was said to have been erected in 1655 and enlarged a century later. It remains uncertain whether the lower stage of the tower is post-medieval Gothic work of 1655, or a late medieval tower retained from a still earlier chapel.

HEMSWORTH
St Helen

A church consisting of a three-bay aisled nave with west tower and south porch, and a chancel with a two-bay south chapel and a north vestry and organ chamber. The visible medieval remains suggest that a nave of uncertain date received a handsome new chancel, with a south chapel, in the second quarter of the 14th century (the tracery of their east windows is the only medieval work visible on the external elevations); the nave arcades look to be 15th century. Everything else is Victorian. On the floor of the south chapel is an unusual early 15th-century slab with incised busts of a man and wife shown above floriated crosses; there are some good post-medieval wall monuments. *See also* **77, 78**.

HEPTONSTALL
The Old Church of St Thomas Becket

Heptonstall old church, now a roofless shell, consists of a four-bay nave and a two-bay chancel each with south aisle, a broad north aisle (or north nave/ north chancel) and an outer north aisle, along with a west tower and south porch. The building has had a long and complicated history: an aisleless 12th or 13th-century church had a west tower added in the 13th century, then nave aisles (and the south porch) early in the 15th century, followed by a rebuilding of the chancel with the addition of flanking chapels. The tower was heightened around 1440. It would appear that a major extension took place in the late 16th or early 17th century, when the north aisle and chapel were rebuilt to their present dimensions, and the outer north aisle added. Both nave arcades were rebuilt at this time, the stonework from the old arcades being used to make the new one opening into the outer aisle. In the 17th century gables with mullioned and transomed windows were raised on the nave and north aisle walls to give light to galleries. The church was abandoned after the new church on the south side of the churchyard was built in 1854; it remains a prime example of a Pennine chapel of uncertain origins which developed into a building larger than many parish churches. *See also* pp 45, 82; **71, 72, 129, 130, 134**.

HORBURY
St Peter and St Leonard

A chapelry of Wakefield which had an ancient chapel pulled down in 1790, to be replaced by an impressive Classical church designed by John Carr and built, at his own expense, as a *natale monumentum*. The drawing is based upon a surviving illustration of the old building, which shows it as having a lofty west tower slightly reminiscent of Bardsey, and a nave and chancel with what the Victorians would have termed 'debased' windows and, on the nave, roof dormers to light galleries. All that survive now are a capital and a fragment of window tracery in the vicarage garden, and two slightly coped cross slabs of *c*. 1300 lying outside the north door of the present church. *See also* p. 89.

HUDDERSFIELD
St Peter

The old parish church of Huddersfield, shown above, was demolished in 1834-35. It consisted of a four-bay aisled nave with a west tower, and a two-bay aisled chancel; it seems to have been largely of 15th and early 16th-century date. All that was retained in its successor, which is still very much a 'preaching box' (retaining all its galleries), is the unusual font carved with the Royal Arms and dated 1570, and a few 17th-century grave slabs. *See also* **124, 146, 147**.

ILKLEY
All Saints

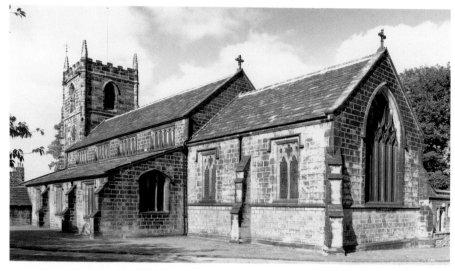

Ilkley parish church, standing on the site of a Roman fort, now consists of a four-bay aisled nave with a west tower and south porch, and a chancel with a north chapel and vestries. The oldest surviving fabric, of uncertain date, is in the west wall of the nave; this early nave seems to have been widened to the south before the present aisles and tower were built in the 15th century, the south aisle reusing a 13th-century doorway. In 1861 the nave was lengthened one bay to the east, and the eastern parts of the church rebuilt; there were further extensions in 1927. The church contains many items of interest: in the base of the tower are three fine Anglo-Saxon crosses, two Roman altars which had been reused as Anglo-Saxon window heads, and a Roman inscription. Other carved stones from the church are in the nearby Manor House Museum. The fine effigy of Sir Peter Middleton (d. 1336) lies in the 1927 north chapel. *See also* pp 9, 10; **10, 11, 12**.

KEIGHLEY
St Andrew

The present Keighley parish church is entirely a building of 1848, designed by R.D. Chantrell (see Leeds, St Peter). The only older relics are four cross slabs set in the walls of the south aisle, a few post-medieval monuments and a '1661' font.

KIPPAX
St Mary

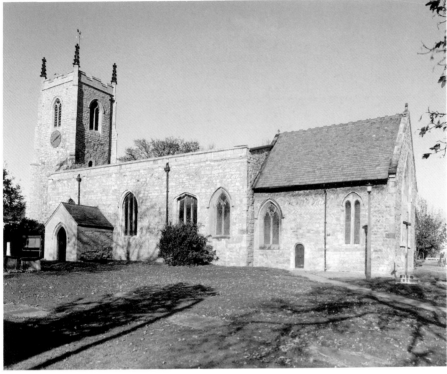

A prominent hilltop landmark, this church is of simple plan – nave with west tower and south porch, chancel with 19th-century north vestry – but quite large dimensions. It seems likely that the body of the church, with its spectacular display of herringbone fabric, belongs to the few years around 1100 when Kippax was an important administrative centre, and when the adjacent ringwork castle was built. The poor condition of the architectural features of the original fabric can be ascribed to the effects of a serious fire in about 1300; in the subsequent reconstruction new windows and a triple piscina were inserted in the chancel and a pair of new doorways in the nave. The belfry was rebuilt in the 15th century (there is a 1430 bequest to the fabric of the tower) and again in the late 19th century when the church was restored. The south porch may be of 17th-century date; its timber-framed front was unfortunately replaced by stonework in 1960. Inside the church are a two pieces of a late Anglo-Saxon cross shaft, and a '1663' font; in the churchyard 20m east of the chancel lies an ornate 14th-century cross slab of the small 'graveyard' group (compare Ackworth, Darrington and Methley). *See also* pp 26, 47; **32, 75, 76**.

KIRKBURTON
All Hallows

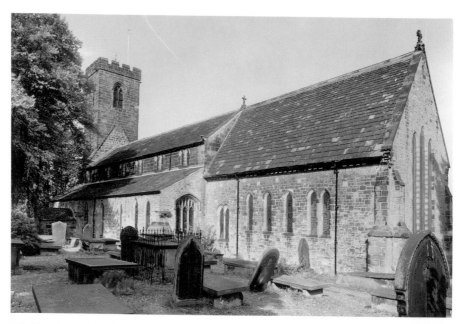

Kirkburton church stands in a striking position on the end of a spur; the building has a six-bay aisled nave with a west tower, north and south porches, and a chancel with north vestry and organ chamber. Some masonry survives of the unaisled nave of 12th-century date (or perhaps earlier) which preceded a major 13th-century remodelling; this left the church with its present plan, except for the 15th-century tower, the 19th-century porches and the 1907 vestry and organ chamber. The best 13th-century features are the nave arcades and the west doorway reset in the tower; there was a considerable amount of alteration in the 'gallery' period of the 18th and early 19th centuries, as evidenced by blocked windows in the south aisle and the 1825 rebuilding of the north aisle. The chancel was rebuilt, more or less on its original lines, in 1850. In the nave is a 10th or early 11th-century stone crucifix; the nave retains its late 16th and 17th-century pewing, a rare survival. In the large and rambling churchyard are various piles of architectural fragments and worked stones from the church, some medieval. *See also* pp 24, 38, 40; **58-63**.

KIRKHEATON
St John

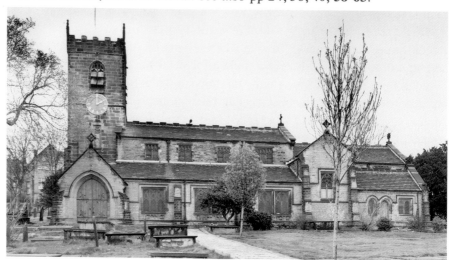

Kirkheaton church is sited at the junction of three out of the four townships within the parish, rather than in Kirkheaton village which is some distance away. The medieval structure, which had been partly rebuilt in 1823, was largely destroyed by fire in 1886; only the 15th-century west tower and 14th or 15th-century Beaumont Chapel (on the north side of the chancel) were retained in the present building. The Beaumont Chapel contains a number of interesting 17th and 18th-century monuments; there is also a simple font of late 11th or early 12th-century date, and a few pieces of post-medieval woodwork that survived the fire. A number of Anglo-Saxon and medieval carved stones, have been removed to the Tolson Memorial Museum in Huddersfield. These include an interesting Anglo-Saxon window head, part of a 9th or 10th-century cross shaft, and a stone inscribed with runic letters. *See also* **31, 125-128**.

KIRKTHORPE
St Peter

In its present form Kirkthorpe (or Warmfield) parish church has a nave with a four-bay north aisle, west tower, south porch and north-west vestry, and a chancel with a three-bay north chapel. The three western bays of the nave seem to be of 12th-century date (some areas of typically 'Norman' masonry survive, along with part of the rear arch of the original south door); the other medieval features of the building mostly relate to a 15th-century remodelling. The vestry, in its unusual position, may have been added in 1688 (a worn datestone survives). In 1850-51 the church was 'almost rebuilt' at a cost of £1,300; both nave and chancel were extended eastwards by an extra bay, and most of the external walls refaced. Both nave and chancel have arcades with quatrefoil piers; it is now very difficult to distinguish between the genuine medieval and the 19th-century work. There are some fine post-medieval monuments in the church, notably two on the south side of the chancel, to Thomas and Katherine Stringer (d. 1681/1707) and to Sir Charles Dalston (d. 1723), which have recently been conserved. *See also* p. 94.

KNOTTINGLEY
St Botolph

Formerly a chapel in the parish of Ferry Fryston, the present church at Knottingley consists of a broad 'preaching box' nave with a west tower, south porch, and a chancel with a north vestry and organ chamber. Render without and plaster within conceal the wall surfaces, and so it is difficult to do more than guess at the structural history of the building. A medieval nave was rebuilt and widened (possibly by incorporating a former south aisle) in 1750; a short 18th-century chancel was extended in 1887, and a west tower, possibly early 19th century, was heightened in 1873. The only ancient feature visible is a blocked window (only visible internally) in the west wall of the original nave; this is round-headed and seems to be of 12th-century date.

LEDSHAM
All Saints

Almost certainly the oldest standing building in West Yorkshire, Ledsham church now consists of a nave with a three-bay north aisle, west tower and south porch, and a chancel with a two-bay north chapel and 19th-century north vestry. The walls of the nave, the lower part of the tower (formerly a west porch), and possibly also the south porch represent an Anglo-Saxon church of around AD 700; although many archaeologists and architectural historians have examined the building, it still requires further study. The west porch may have been raised into a tower in the late Anglo-Saxon period, although its present belfry is mid-12th-century work (compare Aberford and Bramham). In the 13th century the chancel was rebuilt, and in the 15th century the north aisle and then the north chapel added, the tower receiving its embattled parapet and stone spire at about the same time. In the 1871 restoration the chancel was largely rebuilt and the decorative carving on the Anglo-Saxon tower door recut. The Anglo-Saxon features of the church – the tower door, windows in the tower and nave walls, and the chancel arch – are all of national importance, but there is much of interest in the medieval features as well, and in the 17th and 18th-century monuments in the chancel chapel. *See also* pp 15, 16; **3, 7, 8, 9, 18, 19, 20, 43, 153**.

**LEEDS
St Peter**

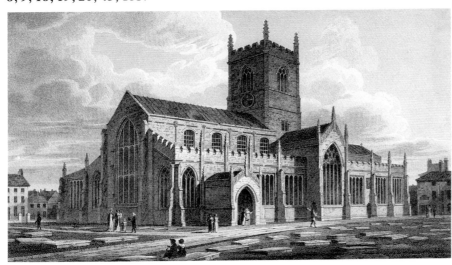

The old parish church of St Peter, seen in the drawing above, was a cruciform building with a four-bay nave, a crossing tower, transepts, and a three-bay chancel; both nave and chancel had north, south, and outer north aisles, and there was a small vestry at the east end. The church appears to have been a building of 13th to 15th-century date; it was demolished in 1838 and replaced by the present building designed by R. Dennis Chantrell. Many pieces of Anglo-Saxon crosses were found incorporated in the fabric of the old church; Chantrell reconstructed one near-complete cross with carvings that mix Christian and pagan Scandinavian themes. Medieval brasses, a 14th-century effigy, and a large number of post-medieval monuments have also been preserved, along with a carved 15th-century font. The churchyard has been bisected by both a road and a railway, and decaying grave slabs, some as early as the beginning of the 17th century, are laid down as paving and even used to revet the sides of the railway embankment. *See also* **16, 142**.

**LOTHERTON
HALL CHAPEL**

Formerly a chapel-of-ease in the parish of Sherburn (now in North Yorkshire), this is a small nave and chancel building which is basically of late 12th-century date (although there are hints that there may in fact be two or more phases of Norman work). The north door is a good specimen of Transitional work, still with a round arch but with mouldings and capitals which show Gothic influences. The original windows are very small, with the simplest of incised line decoration on their heads. The bell-cote may be 13th or 14th century, although the west gable on which it stands seems to have been taken down and rebuilt when the nave was shortened by 1.50m, probably in the 18th century. The priest's door and two large mullioned windows may be late medieval or even post-medieval work. The king-post roof of the chancel looks 15th century; the nave has collar-beam trusses which may be post-medieval. *See also* p. 30; **153**.

**METHLEY
St Oswald**

Methley church consists of a nave with a three-bay south aisle, a west tower, south porch, and a chancel with a two-bay south chapel and a north vestry and organ chamber. The north wall of the nave is probably a 13th-century rebuild on older foundations (the footings of an older cross-wall can be seen by lifting a trapdoor in the nave floor); the south aisle was added in the 14th century at the expense of two brothers whose effigies (once parts of the same tomb) lie in tomb recesses in nave and aisle. The chancel may have been rebuilt at the same time; the Waterton Chapel on its south side was probably built in 1483-84; the west tower, nave clerestory and nave roof are probably of 15th-century date as well. The chancel was extended and the vestry block built in the later 19th century; these extensions were rebuilt again in 1925-26. The church contains many monuments and furnishings of interest; there are several medieval and post-medieval tombs with effigies, a 15th-century font with a cover of 1584, a medieval screen in the Waterton Chapel and important 15th-century glass in the chapel east window. *See also* p. 71; **113**.

MIRFIELD
St Mary

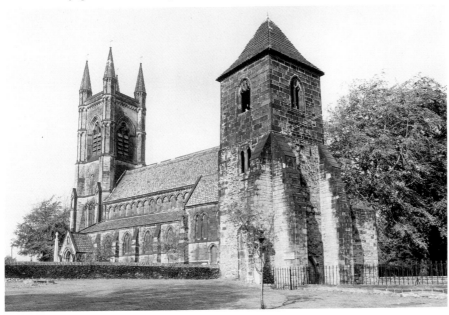

The old parish church of Mirfield consisted of a nave with a four-bay north aisle, west tower, south porch, and a chancel with a north chapel or vestry. The tower and aisle appear to have been 13th-century additions to a slightly older nave; the tower was given a new belfry in the 15th century (compare Heptonstall). The north aisle was rebuilt and enlarged in 1666 to hold a gallery for the owners of Over Hall. In 1826 the whole body of the church was rebuilt, on the old external walls, as a preaching box. When the present parish church was built in 1871 by Sir George Gilbert Scott, the old building was pulled down except for the tower and west wall of the nave (the embattled top of the tower was replaced by a pyramidal roof supposedly in keeping with its 13th-century parts), and the lower courses of its walls which now enclose a Garden of Rest. The surviving tower and west wall preserve a variety of features which demonstrate the history of the building, and are worth a detailed study. Inside the 'new' church is a late Anglo-Saxon headstone. *See also* pp 44-45; **73**.

NORMANTON
All Saints

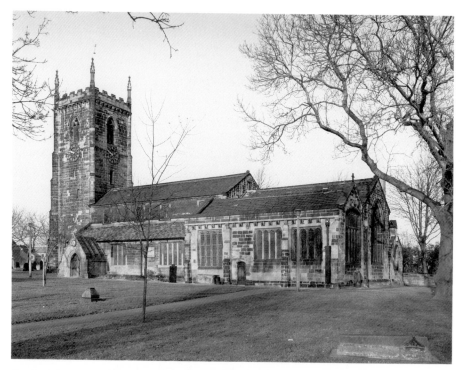

A church consisting of a four-bay aisled nave with a west tower, south porch and a north vestry, and a chancel with a three-bay south chapel and a north vestry and organ chamber. The nave walls may be 11th century or even earlier; the north aisle is a mid-13th-century addition and the chancel may have been rebuilt at this time as well. The south aisle (and porch) may be 14th century and the west tower is of the usual later 15th-century form. The chancel chapel is early 16th-century work with typical 'Tudor' windows. In the 19th century the chancel and south aisle were largely rebuilt, and both vestries added. There are some interesting post-medieval monuments in the church, and a puzzling font that might be 15th century. There is a large amount of old glass, but most of this was imported in the 19th century. *See also* **91, 96**.

OTLEY
All Saints

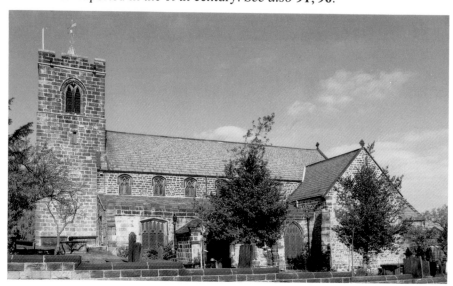

Otley parish church consists of a four-bay nave with a tower, south porch and transepts, and a chancel with north and south vestries. The earliest visible masonry is in the 12th-century chancel, but it seems possible that the nave – of unusually large dimensions – is earlier. The transepts may be 13th century (although their diagonal buttresses look later medieval in style), and the west tower and refacing of the west end of the nave are 14th-century work. The nave aisles may be 15th-century additions, although the north aisle incorporates a late 12th-century door. Unfortunately the Victorians dealt harshly with the church; their recutting of stonework, and the present plastering of the internal walls, has doubtless obscured much evidence. The church has the best collection of Anglo-Saxon sculpture in the county. *See also* pp 22-23; **51**.

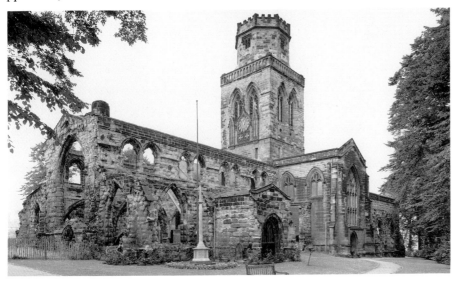

PONTEFRACT
All Saints

All Saints, the old parish church of Pontefract, consisted of a four-bay aisled nave with north and south porches, a central tower, transepts (that on the north having two eastern chapels), and a chancel with a three-bay south chapel and a north-east vestry. The core of the nave and chancel is probably 12th or 13th century; there was a major series of building campaigns in the first half of the 14th century when the chancel was remodelled, the transepts and tower (with its rare double-helix stair) built, and the nave aisles (and porches) added. The Lady Chapel on the south side of the chancel (replacing the south transept's smaller eastern chapels) and the octagon crowning the tower seem to have been later 14th-century additions. Later in the medieval period, walls were heightened, new windows inserted and the vestry built. Then in 1644-45 the church suffered through its over-active involvement in the drama of the Civil War sieges of the nearby castle, and was reduced to a roofless ruin. The damaged octagon collapsed soon after and was rebuilt (on a smaller scale) late in the 17th century. In 1831 R. Dennis Chantrell refurbished the crossing and transepts (and added a small sanctuary within the ruined chancel) to serve as a chapel-of-ease to St Giles, which had become the parish church in 1789; in 1967 a new nave (within the medieval arcades) was added to designs by G.G. Pace. *See also* pp 50-51; **83**.

PONTEFRACT
St Giles

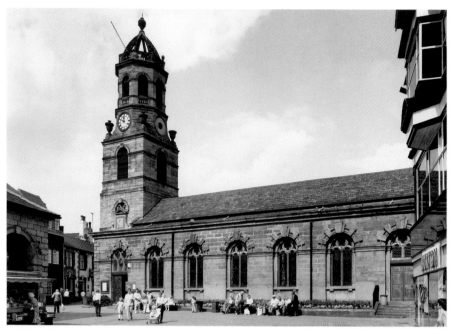

Once 'St Mary de Foro' (St Mary in the Market Place), St Giles is thought to have originated as a 12th-century chapel-of-ease to All Saints, although their roles are now reversed. The church has a five-bay aisled nave with a west tower, a single-bay aisled chancel, and a sanctuary with a vestry on the south. The only visible medieval work is the north arcade of around 1300, with quatrefoil piers, and the panelled nave ceiling (?15th century). The tower was rebuilt in 1707 and again in 1790-91, the south arcade and aisle in 1740, the west part of the chancel in 1792, and the sanctuary (the east part of the medieval chancel) in 1868-69, when the Classical windows of the church received their incongruous Gothic tracery. There is a 15th-century font (from All Saints).

ROTHWELL
Holy Trinity

A church consisting of a five-bay aisled nave with a west tower and south porch, and a chancel with a three-bay north aisle, north vestry and south organ chamber. Extensive 19th-century rebuilding has destroyed any visible evidence of the church as it existed before the usual 15th-century remodelling; from this the west tower, a good panelled nave ceiling with carved bosses (rediscovered in 1841; it had been underdrawn and plastered), the south doorway (with its original door), and a little walling in the south aisle are the only survivals. The south porch may be of 17th-century date. In 1826 the chancel and north aisle were rebuilt; the vestry may have been built in 1843, the chancel was gothicised in 1849, the organ chamber added in 1866, the north nave arcade reinstated in 1873, and the south arcade and aisle rebuilt in 1892. Recent (1988) alterations to the vestry revealed (and destroyed) a plain round-arched window with a keystone in the chancel north wall. *See also* pp 93-94; **94, 103, 144, 145**.

SANDAL MAGNA
St Helen

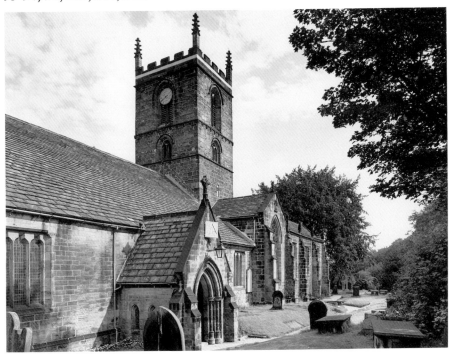

This is a cruciform church with a six-bay aisled nave, south porch, central tower, transepts, and a chancel with a four-bay south chapel and north vestries and organ chamber. The oldest parts of the building – the lower parts of the crossing and some masonry in at least the south transept – may be late Anglo-Saxon, and reused bases and a capital indicate that at least one aisle was added to the nave in the late 12th century. There was a general rebuilding in the early 14th century, leaving the church much as we see it today, except that the tower was heightened by the addition of a new belfry in the 15th century, the south chancel chapel was rebuilt to its present size in about 1505, and the nave was lengthened westwards by two bays in 1872. In addition there is some evidence that the nave arcades were reconstructed in the 17th or 18th century to facilitate the insertion of galleries; the present vestries are 19th and 20th century. *See also* pp 18-20, 48-49; **26, 27, 79, 154**.

SOUTH KIRKBY
All Saints

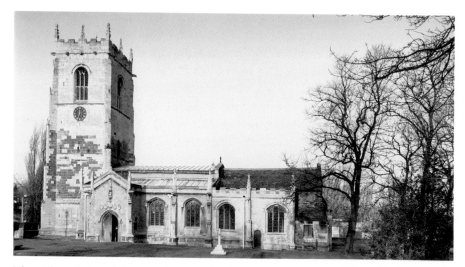

The *Cherchebi* of Domesday Book, South Kirkby has an interesting church now consisting of a two-bay aisled nave, west tower, south porch, and a two-bay aisled chancel with a sacristy at the east end of its south chapel. The Perpendicular exterior, as often, belies a long and complex building history. Anglo-Saxon or very early Norman walling survives at the four corners of the nave; the rather wider chancel is obviously a rebuild, and this seems 12th century (see the masonry and a blocked window on the north). The nave aisles appear to have been built (or rebuilt) soon after 1200; the north chancel chapel seems to have been added later in the 13th century. Then in the 15th century came the usual remodelling, with the addition of the west tower and the rebuilding of most of the external walls. The nave walls seem to have been taken down and rebuilt, with two-bay instead of three-bay arcades, during the 'gallery period' of the late 17th or 18th century. *See also* pp 59, 64, 84, 86; **93, 101, 133**.

SWILLINGTON
St Mary

A church with a five-bay aisled nave, west tower, south porch, and a chancel with north vestry and organ chamber. The walls of the nave (see the western quoins, and a blocked window cut by the north arcade) are probably 12th century; the aisles and chancel date from a late 14th-century remodelling. The west tower is a typical mid-15th-century specimen, although it was reclad in gritstone in 1884 (with a few minor 'improvements' in detail). With years of atmospheric pollution the gritstone has blackened, whilst the magnesian limestone body of the church remains off-white, a strange tonal contrast. In the north aisle, at the west end of the internal face of the north wall, is a reset 12th-century window head with an incised pattern of saltire crosses; there is a similar but undecorated stone reused at the south end of the east wall of the chancel. There are several medieval monuments, including fragments of a wooden effigy, now set in a case in the good 14th-century tomb recess in the south aisle. *See also* p. 52; **4**.

THORNER
St Peter

Thorner parish church has a three-bay aisled nave with a west tower and south porch, and a chancel with two-bay side chapels and a mid-20th-century north vestry. The mid-15th-century west tower is built onto the west wall of what seems to have been an aisleless nave, but this retains no datable features; the nave arcades look 15th century as well, although detail differences suggest they result from separate building campaigns. The medieval church had an aisleless chancel, and was remodelled in the late 18th or early 19th century with 'pseudo-Italian' windows (as happened at Rothwell). In 1855 the church was restored; the south aisle, porch, and eastern parts were entirely rebuilt. The nave roof, 'a most massive and striking specimen of medieval carpentry', was replaced. *See also* **97**.

THORNHILL
St Michael and
All Angels

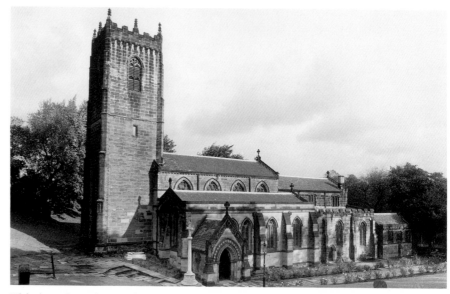

This is quite a large church, consisting of a four-bay aisled nave with a west tower and a south porch, and a three-bay chancel with side chapels and a south-east vestry. Later rebuildings of the nave have removed all clear evidence of pre-15th-century work in the church, although there are some hints and traces in the tower and in the west wall of the north chancel chapel. The present tower is mostly 15th century, and the fine collection of medieval glass gives us dates for the various eastern parts: the north (Savile) chapel added in 1447 then lengthened by a bay in 1493, the south chapel added in 1491, and the chancel 'clerstoried and archyde' (and the east window inserted) in 1499. The nave was rebuilt as a 'preaching box' in 1777, and again (this time in a 14th-century Gothic style) exactly 100 years later. Apart from the glass there is much else of interest: in the north aisle is an important collection of Anglo-Saxon carved stones, some with inscriptions; there are three medieval tombs with effigies, and a considerable number of post-medieval monuments. *See also* pp 72, 89; **90, 114, 115, 116, 140**.

THORP ARCH
All Saints

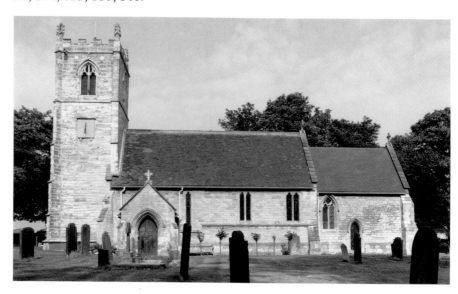

The church consists of a nave with a three-bay north aisle, west tower, south porch, and a chancel with a north organ chamber and vestry. On the strength of the surviving south door the medieval church seems to have had a 12th-century nave. The chancel seems to have been rebuilt in the 13th or 14th century and the tower was added in the 15th century; the north aisle may have been a late medieval addition. In 1756-62 there was a general remodelling in a style later described as 'Carpenter's Gothic'; the building was remodelled again in 1871-72 in a medieval style more fitting to Victorian taste. Of the medieval church there survives the tower, the south door (which between the 18th and 19th-century works had been set in the west wall of the tower), some masonry in the south wall of the nave, and parts of the chancel with a (restored) tomb recess and piscina. There are some interesting carved stones, including part of an Anglo-Saxon cross, built into the walls of the porch.

TODMORDEN
St Mary

This town centre church consists of a broad 'preaching box' nave, west tower, south porch, and a chancel with south vestry and organ chamber. Originally a chapel in the parish of Rochdale, the early history of the building is obscure. The lower part of the tower may be late medieval, or late 16th/early 17th century (there was formerly a '1603' bell). The present nave was rebuilt in 1770 by Anthony Crossley, with galleries on north, east and west (only the western one now remains); the north wall seems to incorporate older masonry, possibly from a former north aisle. The present Gothic chancel is of 1896; it was planned to rebuild the nave at the same time, but fortunately this was never carried out. *See also* p. 88.

175

TONG
St James

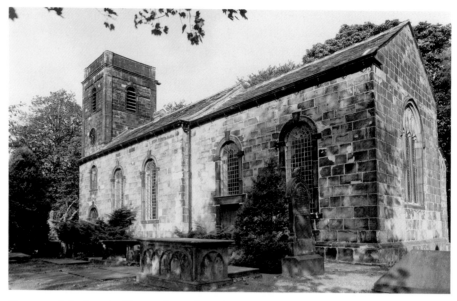

Tong parish church (formerly a chapel to Birstall) has a nave with a three-bay north aisle, west tower, south porch, and a chancel with a north vestry and organ chamber. Excavations by the West Yorkshire Archaeology Service in the early 1980s showed that the present building, a 1727 rebuilding by Sir George Tempest, overlies a simple two-cell church thought to be of 12th-century date. Nothing of this survives above ground except for reused masonry and a reset arch, probably originally the chancel arch but now opening into the tower. The church has an excellent early 18th-century interior with box pews, three-decker pulpit, Tempest family pew, altar rails, panelled dado and west gallery. *See also* pp 87, 88, Chapter Twelve.

WAKEFIELD
The Cathedral
Church of
All Saints

Wakefield Cathedral, formerly the parish church of All Saints, consists of a nave with a seven-bay north aisle and an eight-bay south aisle, west tower, south porch, a chancel with five-bay aisles, and an early 20th-century eastern arm with transepts and chapels; there are various 19th and 20th-century vestries on the north. Masonry in the nave walls and south chancel aisle is interpreted as representing an aisleless cruciform church of the early 12th century, to which a north aisle is thought to have been added *c*. 1150 and a south aisle *c*. 1220. Use of the church seems to have been interrupted, perhaps by the fall of the crossing tower, early in the 14th century, when the building was remodelled and the present arcades constructed, reusing older material (as at Sandal Magna). The west tower and spire were built in the first quarter of the 15th century; the nave clerestory was added in the middle of that century, followed by the rebuilding of the whole eastern arm, and then by the widening of the nave aisles and the addition of porches. The plan thus became a fully aisled rectangle as shown in the accompanying early 19th-century illustration, the projection of the early transepts having been absorbed by the widening of the nave aisles. The external walls on the south were rebuilt or refaced around 1725, and those on the north later in the 18th century. The main 19th-century restoration was carried out by Sir George Gilbert Scott in 1858-74, and involved much refacing and remedievalisation of windows and other features altered in the preceding century. The eastern extensions, designed by F.L. Pearson, are of 1901-05, built following the elevation of the old parish church to its new status. The nave and chancel retain their late medieval panelled ceilings. The fittings and furnishings include much of interest. *See also* pp 48, 65, 74-75, 89, 98-100; **118**.

**WAKEFIELD
The Bridge
Chantry**

A small but highly ornate rectangular chapel, built around 1350 on an island in the River Calder adjacent to the medieval bridge. This most ornate piece of Decorated Gothic in West Yorkshire can be seen in the 18th-century illustration above, but sadly the building we see today is no more than a mid-19th-century copy of the original; genuine medieval stonework survives only in the basement sacristy. The old west front, much eroded, now forms the facade of a boat house at Kettlethorpe Hall. *See also* pp 52, 54; **88**.

WALTON
St Peter

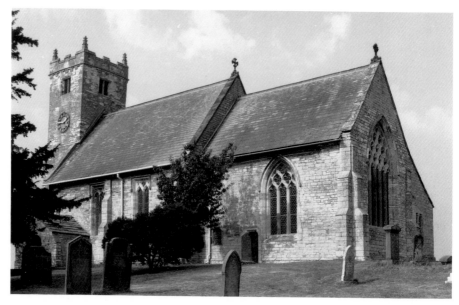

This is probably the best small 14th-century church in West Yorkshire, and was originally a chapel-of-ease to Thorp Arch. The church consists of an aisleless nave, west tower, south porch, and a chancel with north vestry and organ chamber. Apart from a plain early Norman arch to the tower (perhaps an earlier chancel arch reset), the belfry stage of the tower, the 18th-century porch and the organ chamber and vestry of 1890-91, the entire building is of *c.* 1340-50, with some good reticulated tracery in its windows. There have been 'low-side' windows on both sides of the chancel, the northern being reset in the organ chamber. Inside there is a fine contemporary tomb recess in the chancel, holding a knight's effigy of the later 14th century, and a late medieval font. All three bells are of about 1500, and the bell-frames (possibly from an all-timber belfry remodelled when the present bells were hung) are medieval – a rare survival in this area. *See also* p. 52; **84-87**, **154**.

WHITKIRK
St Mary

178

A parish church consisting of a four-bay aisled nave with a west tower and south porch, and a chancel with a two-bay south chapel, a one-bay north chapel and north-east vestry. Almost all of the present church is of mid-15th-century date; the chancel, rebuilt and extended in 1900-01, may have been a century or so earlier. At the eastern angles of the nave single massive piers (compare Halifax, Wragby and elsewhere) carry the chancel arch, nave and chancel arcades, and the arches between nave aisles and chancel chapels. The tower is one of a distinctive group with diagonal buttresses and corbelled-out parapets (others include Barwick, Rothwell, Swillington and Thorner). There are several interesting medieval and post-medieval monuments, including the mid-16th-century Scargill tomb with its alabaster effigies and a tablet to John Smeaton, the famous 18th-century engineer, showing the Eddystone lighthouse. *See also* p. 70; **112**.

WOODKIRK
St Mary

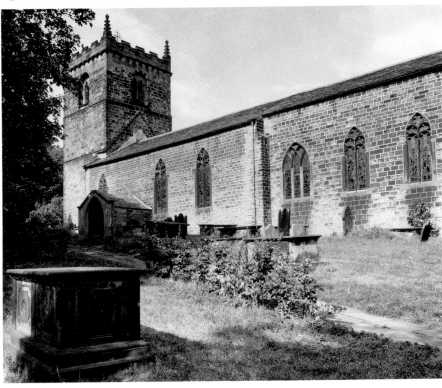

Woodkirk is thought to be the Domesday church of 'St Mary in the Wood of Morlege'; it later served a small Augustinian priory, a dependency of Nostell. The present church is a long and narrow building consisting of an aisleless nave and chancel with a west tower, south porch, and north-east vestry. The medieval building may have had a north aisle; the priory buildings (located by excavation in the 1960s) seem to have been arranged round a cloister on the north. The west tower is of about 1200, and the exposed footings of the chancel later 13th century; the body of the present church was rebuilt between 1831-34, reusing several medieval windows and perhaps incorporating *in situ* the jambs of the chancel arch. There are fine late medieval choir stalls, and a ?17th-century font; outside the south door is a cross base which may well be Anglo-Saxon. *See also* pp 43-44; **68-70**.

WOOLLEY
St Peter

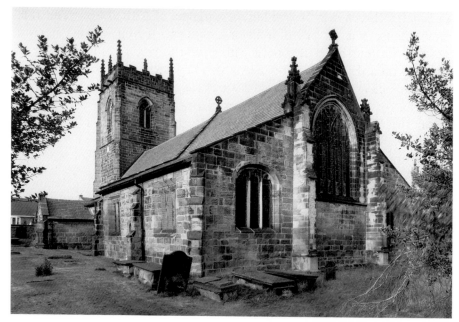

A church having a four-bay aisled nave with a west tower and south porch, and a chancel with three-bay chapels. The structural history of the church is difficult to interpret. The nave walls may be 12th century, the chancel 13th century and the north chapel 14th century, but the only architectural features to survive from these periods are all reset in later walls. Everything else is the product of a comprehensive late 15th and early 16th-century remodelling, carried out in a number of phases. There was an 1870 restoration by Ewan Christian when the floors were lowered and the east end, among other parts, was rebuilt. The rood stair in the south aisle wall reuses a tympanum, carved with the *Agnus Dei*, and a spirally fluted shaft, both probably originating in a 12th-century south door. There are four windows with good late medieval glass. *See also* **53**.

WRAGBY
St Michael

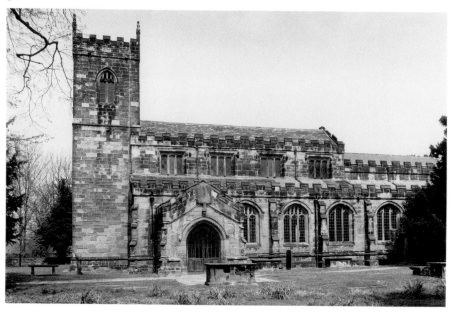

An isolated church standing within the parkland of Nostell Priory, an 18th-century house near the site of a major monastery of Augustinian canons. It consists of a four-bay aisled nave with a west tower, a south porch, and a chancel with a three-bay north aisle, a two-bay south aisle and a south-east vestry. The panelled ceiling of the chancel has an inscription asking prayers for the soul of Alured Comyn, last Prior of Nostell, and the date 1533; it would appear that the whole church was rebuilt at this date in a fairly plain Perpendicular style except for the west end of the nave and the ?early 15th-century west tower; the evidence of the plinths suggests that there was an intention to replace this rather humble tower, but presumably Henry VIII and the Dissolution intervened. Many of the furnishings and fittings of the church are 18th and 19th-century imports, including a large amount of old stained glass (mostly Swiss). At the time of writing the glass is 'in store' and the fabric of the church under some threat due to coal mining beneath the site. *See also* p. 67; **106**.

a *Plan showing the principal elements of a medieval church*

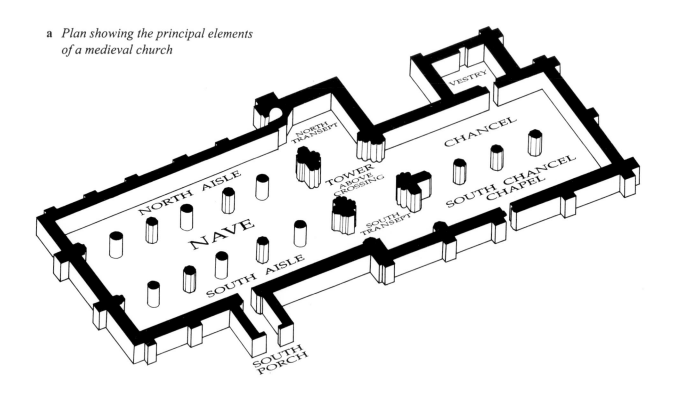

VESTRY

NORTH AISLE

NORTH TRANSEPT

CHANCEL

TOWER ABOVE CROSSING

NAVE

SOUTH CHANCEL CHAPEL

SOUTH TRANSEPT

SOUTH AISLE

SOUTH PORCH

b *Typical architectural features of a parish church*

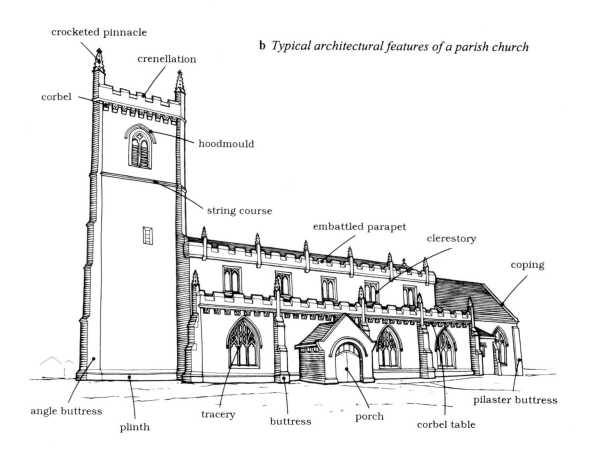

crocketed pinnacle

crenellation

corbel

hoodmould

string course

embattled parapet

clerestory

coping

angle buttress

plinth

tracery

buttress

porch

corbel table

pilaster buttress

Glossary

Letters in brackets refer to drawings

Abacus. The flat slab forming the uppermost member of a capital, from which the arch springs. (l)

Anglo-Saxon. A broad term covering all architecture in England between the Romans and the Norman Conquest; sometimes described as pre-Norman Romanesque.

Arcade. A series of columns and arches separating, for instance, a nave and aisles or a chancel and its side chapels. (l)

Ashlar. Good-quality masonry with regularly cut, smooth-faced blocks.

Aumbry. Small cupboard-like recess, sometimes rebated for a door, in which the sacramental vessels were stored close to an altar.

Beakhead. A carving of a grotesque bird-like head, typically on the voussoir of a Norman doorway.

Belfry. The uppermost stage of a tower, containing the bellframes and bells.

Bone hole. Vault, crypt or cellar used to store bones removed from the churchyard.

Boss. Carved projecting ornament of wood or stone, often at the intersection of the ribs of a vault or panelled ceiling. (i)

Broach stop. One form of chamfer stop, resembling a steep pyramid or spire.

Buttress. Projection acting to support or stabilise a wall. (b)

Capital. Feature forming the head of a column.

Chantry. Chapel, usually within a church, founded specifically as a place where Masses could be said for the soul of a benefactor.

Cinquefoil. Panel divided into five by cusping, i.e. in tracery, or as the head of an arch. (c)

Classical. Style and decoration associated with Greek and Roman architecture.

Clerestory. A range of windows high in the side wall of the nave or chancel of a church, usually above the aisle roof. (b)

Cloister. Usually associated with a monastic house; an open court adjacent to the church, surrounded by a covered walkway.

Collar-beam. Horizontal member of a truss, linking the two principal rafters midway between the apex and the wall-plate.

183

Collared rafter. A type of roof in which there are no separate trusses, but each pair of rafters is of similar scantling, linked and strengthened by a horizontal member or collar.

Coping. Course of dressed or moulded stone topping a wall. (b)

Corbel. Piece of stone or wood, usually shaped, projecting from the wall face to carry the end of a beam or an arch. (b)

Crenellation. A battlemented parapet or wall top, or a smaller-scale version of battlements used as an ornament. (b)

Crocket. Knob-like ornament, usually carved in the form of a leaf, on the steep side of a pinnacle or spire, e.g. crocketed pinnacles. (b)

Cross slab. The most common form of medieval sepulchral monument to survive; a horizontal slab carved with a cross and, often, some emblem representing the trade of the deceased person.

Cusp. Projecting point formed at the intersection of two arcs in Gothic arches and, in particular, the heads of windows.

Decorated. The second of the three English divisions of the Gothic style, in use *c.* 1290-1350, and characterised by the development of window tracery and the carving of naturalistic foliage. (c)

Diaper work. Surface decoration consisting of a repeated pattern of lozenges or squares.

Dog-tooth. Typical Early English moulding consisting of a series of small pyramids each made up of four leaf- or tooth-like motifs. (e)

Early English. The first of the three English divisions of the Gothic style, in vogue throughout the 13th century, and characterised by pointed arches, lancet windows, and ornaments such as dog-tooth and nail-head. (d)

Extrados. The outer curve of an arch or vault. (l)

Gablet. Small gable used ornamentally.

Gallery. A partial upper floor or loft, almost always of wood, often inserted into a church in the 18th or early 19th century to provide extra accommodation.

Geometrical tracery. The earliest form of Gothic window tracery, using simple repeating patterns such as circles, trefoils and quatrefoils.

Gibbs surround. A 17th or 18th-century door surround in which the mouldings are interrupted by unmoulded blocks, characteristic of the work of James Gibbs (1682-1754).

Gothic. The style of architecture, characterised by the pointed arch, succeeding Norman or Romanesque, and usually divided into three sub-styles: the Early English, Decorated and Perpendicular.

c   Decorated

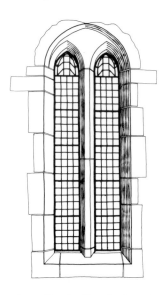

d   Early English

184

Herringbone. Masonry, usually rubble, laid in zig-zag courses; a functional way to create courses of equal height from irregular stones; characteristic of 'Overlap' or early Norman churches.

Hoodmould. Projecting stone moulding carried over the head of an arch, doorway or window. (b, g)

Impost. A horizontal block at the head of a jamb or respond, from which an arch springs. (f)

Intrados. The internal curve or soffit of an arch. (l)

Jacobean. A style of architecture noted for carved woodwork, screens and pulpits, dominant during the reign of James I (1603-25).

Jamb shaft. A small column forming part of the jamb of a window or other opening, often with its own capital and base. (e)

Keystone. A stone, usually raised or accentuated in some way, at the apex of an arch; typical of Classical rather than Gothic architecture.

King-post. In a roof structure, a vertical post rising from the centre of a tie-beam, carrying both the heads of the principal rafters and the ridge. (i)

Lancet window. Tall and narrow window with a pointed arch, typical of the Early English style.

Lewis holes. Rectangular sockets which widen with depth; they are usually evidence of reused Roman masonry. Lifting a stone from a chock secured in the hole with wedges was a common Roman technique.

Lights. The individual divisions of a window, divided by mullions.

Lintel. Horizontal stone or beam spanning an opening.

Lychgate. A roofed gateway, usually of wood, at the entrance to a churchyard, where a coffin could be sheltered (literally 'corpse gate').

Machicolation. A series of openings, often between the corbels, that carry a projecting parapet through which, if need be, objects could be dropped onto unwelcome visitors.

Mullion. Vertical stone or timber member separating the lights of a window. (c)

Nail-head. A moulding consisting of a series of small pyramidal motifs, typical of the Early English style. (e)

Newel. The central pillar of a spiral stair.

Norman. Style of architecture characterised by the round arch and generally heavy and massive proportions, typical of the late 11th and 12th century. Sometimes also referred to as Romanesque (a term sometimes extended backwards to cover Saxon styles as well). (f)

nail-head

jamb shaft   dog-tooth

e

impost

f   Norman

Ogee. A double curve, concave above and convex below; can be used either for the shape of an arch or the profile of a moulding.

Overlap. More fully 'Saxo-Norman Overlap', a term used of churches showing a mixture of both Saxon and Norman features. A few high-status churches (e.g. Waltham Abbey) imported Norman features before the Conquest, but the vast majority date from the century or so after.

Parapet. The upper part of a wall that stands above roof level; often embattled. (b)

Pediment. Used in Classical architecture, a shaped gable-like panel, often triangular, above an opening.

Perpendicular. The third of the English Gothic styles, succeeding the Decorated, and typified by the strong use of vertical lines, large windows, and general lofty proportions. It has been described as the most truly English of the Gothic styles. (g)

Pier. A column or support, usually part of an arcade. (l)

Pilaster. Shallow, rectangular buttress-like feature characteristic of Norman architecture. (b)

Piscina. A recess containing a shallow stone bowl, usually in the wall to the south of an altar; used for washing after the celebration of Mass.

Plate tracery. An early type of tracery, usually of later 13th-century date, in which shaped openings are cut in a single block of stone forming the window head.

Plinth. A projecting course, sometimes chamfered or moulded, at the foot of a wall. (b)

Porticus. Small side chamber or chapel characteristic of Saxon churches; their function remains uncertain.

Principal rafter. The inclined members of a roof truss which usually carry the purlins; sometimes simply known as principals. (i)

Purlin. Horizontal member of the roof structure, midway up the roof slope, carried by the trusses and supporting the rafters. (i)

Quatrefoil. A circle divided into four cusps, usually in window tracery.

Quoins. Or angle quoins; large cut blocks forming the angles of a stone building, especially prominent in Saxon architecture. There are various distinctive types, such as side-alternate and long-and-short. (h, j)

Rafter. Inclined roof timbers, usually of light scantling supported by wall-plate, purlins and ridge, and carrying the actual roofing material. (i)

hoodmould

g   Perpendicular

Quoins

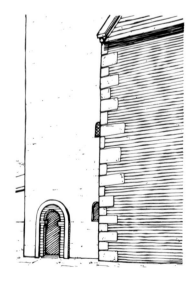

h   side-alternate

186

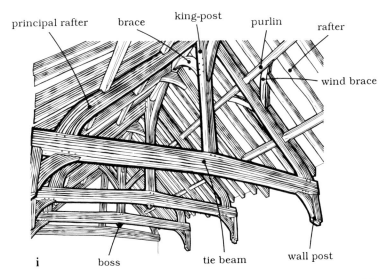

principal rafter brace king-post purlin rafter

wind brace

i boss tie beam wall post

j long-and-short

Renaissance. The reintroduction of Classical and Italian motifs, which took place in English architecture from the mid-16th century onwards, supplanting the Gothic.

Respond. Half-pier set into a wall, carrying an arch.

Reticulated tracery. Tracery consisting of a honeycomb- or net-like pattern of circles drawn out at the top and bottom into ogee shapes.

Ridge (piece). Longitudinal timber at the apex of a roof.

Romanesque. The style of architecture characterised by the round arch, in England more usually termed 'Norman'; some authorities extend its use back to the Anglo-Saxon period as well.

Rood. Large crucifix, generally set within the chancel arch.

Rood beam. Beam, usually set against the west face of a chancel arch, supporting the rood (or crucifix) with attendant statues. A gallery in this position and performing this function is known as the rood loft; access to the beam or loft may be by a rood stair, a small stair often cut through the thickness of the wall at one end.

Rood screen. A carved screen, usually of wood, below the rood loft and separating the chancel from the nave.

Roof loft. A gallery, generally wooden, spanning the west face of the chancel arch above the rood screen, and carrying the rood.

Sacristy. A small room, usually opening off the chancel, used by the priest for robing and storing sacred vessels.

Saltire. Small cross with arms set diagonally (cf. 'St Andrew's Cross').

Sanctuary. The eastern part of the chancel, housing the altar.

Scalloped capital. Common form of Norman capital, usually square, in which the sides are cut into a series of scallops. (l)

Scantling. A term relating to the dimensions of timbers, e.g. light or heavy scantling.

Sedilia. Seats for priests, generally three, usually recessed into the south wall of the chancel close to the altar.

Shouldered arch. An opening in which a lintel is carried on a pair of corbels. (k)

Side-alternate. Usually referring to angle quoins laid on their sides, with the long faces of the stone alternately set along one wall and then the other. (h)

Soffit. The underside of a feature such as an arch or beam.

Spandrel. The roughly triangular space above a pier, between two arches, or between the curve of an arch and the adjacent wall or roof. (l)

k   shouldered arch

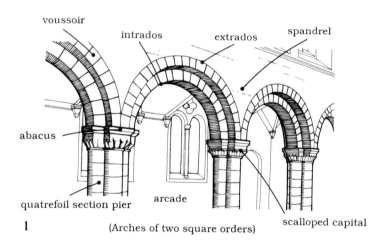

l   (Arches of two square orders)

Splay. The widening, usually internal, from the narrowest section of an opening to the wall face. (c)

Squint. Opening cut through a wall, partition or pier, so that the altar can be seen from a side chapel or aisle.

Stoothing. Partition or wall-casing of timber and plaster.

Stoup. Stone basin set into the wall, to hold holy water, usually beside or just inside a doorway.

Strapwork. Typical 16th or 17th-century decoration, imitating bands of cut leather.

String-course. Projecting horizontal course of stonework, often moulded. (b)

Stripwork. Raised strips of stonework typical of pre-Conquest architecture; often thought to imitate the structural elements of a timber-framed building.

Strut. Usually used in conjunction with timber roof structures; often a short timber, set either vertically or diagonally, linking two members (e.g. tie-beam and principal rafter) of a truss.

Stucco. A coating of fine lime plaster, often painted.

Tie-beam. In a roof structure, the principal horizontal member at the base of a truss, spanning the width of the building. (i)

Tracery. Ornamental ribwork dividing a series of lights, often cusped, in the head of a Gothic window. (b)

Transitional. A period in between two architectural styles; in England it usually refers to the transition between Norman and Early English, *c.* 1150-1200.

Transom. Horizontal stone or timber member dividing the lights of a window.

Trefoil. Panel divided into three by cusping, either in tracery or at the head of an arch. (c)

Truss. An individual cross-frame within a roof structure, carrying the longitudinal members (purlins and ridge), which in turn carry the rafters.

Tudor. Politically, the period between 1485-1603, and also an architectural style which followed on from the Perpendicular, in which Renaissance motifs begin to supplant the Gothic.

Tympanum. The panel between the lintel and arch of a doorway (often found in Norman doorways) which may contain ornamental carving.

Venetian window. A window form found in Classical architecture, in which the two square-headed lights flank a taller central opening beneath a round arch.

Voussoir. Wedge-shaped stone block forming part of an arch. (l)

Wall post. Usually a short timber post carried on a corbel and supporting one end of a tie-beam of the roof. (i)

Wall-plate. A horizontal timber resting on top of a wall, supporting the feet of the rafters.

Wind brace. In a roof structure, a diagonal timber on the plane of the roof slope, set between a principal rafter and a purlin. (i)

Further Reading

Cocke, T., Findley, D., Halsey, R. and Williamson, E., 1989   *Recording a Church: An Illustrated Glossary*, Council for British Archaeology, Practical Handbook 7 (3rd edition)

Morris, J.E., 1923   *The West Riding of Yorkshire* (Little Guide Series), Methuen & Co. (2nd edition)

Morris, R.K., 1983   *The Church in British Archaeology*, Council for British Archaeology Research Report 47

Morris, R.K., 1989   *Churches in the Landscape*, J.M. Dent & Sons

Parsons, D., 1989   *Churches and Chapels: Recording Places of Worship*, Council for British Archaeology, Practical Handbook 8

Pevsner, N. and Radcliffe, E. 1967   *Yorkshire: The West Riding* (Buildings of England Series), Penguin (2nd edition)

Rodwell, W.J., 1986   'Anglo-Saxon church building: aspects of design and construction', in Butler, L.A.S. and Morris, R.K. (eds), *The Anglo-Saxon Church*, Council for British Archaeology Research Report 60, 156-75

Rodwell, W.J., 1989   *Church Archaeology*, English Heritage

Ryder, P.F., 1991   *Medieval Cross Slab Grave Covers in West Yorkshire*, West Yorkshire Archaeology Service

Taylor, H.M. and Taylor, J. 1965   *Anglo-Saxon Architecture*, Vols 1 and 2, Cambridge

Taylor, H.M., 1978   *Anglo-Saxon Architecture,* Vol. 3, Cambridge

Thomas, A.C., 1971   *The Early Christian Archaeology of North Britain*, Oxford

Thomas, A.C., 1981   *Christianity in Roman Britain to AD 500*, London

Index

Compiled by Jeny Marriott

Unless discussed or illustrated in detail, the majority of the more common elements of churches, such as aisles, chancels, naves, vestries, are not separately indexed. Such features of individually named churches may be found under the name of the church (*see* churches).

Figure numbers are given in **bold**; unnumbered figures in the gazetteer are indexed by page.